Praise for this Book:

"Virtual presentations are scary until you know what to do. Wayne Turmel has done more of them and done them better than anyone else in the field. And he's a gifted writer who simplifies the subject, takes the 'scary' out, and with a deft humorous touch, makes the whole thing seem like fun."

Kevin Daley
Founder, Communispond
Author, *Talk Your Way to the Top*

"While the thought of making a presentation makes many squirm, making it virtual turns many confident presenters into beginners again. This book is a game changer for all of us. Whether you are a newbie or a seasoned virtual presenter there is value for you here! Wayne's engaging and fun writing on this increasingly important topic makes it even better. This book is practical, useful, and needed. Buy a copy for yourself—and everyone in your organization who is a presenter!"

Kevin Eikenberry
Author of *Remarkable Leadership: Unleashing Your Leadership Potential One Skill at a Time*

"With his wonderful wit and insanely helpful examples, Wayne Turmel has created a knockout book for anyone who needs to communicate using virtual presentations. Oh, wait, that's everyone, isn't it?"

Lisa Haneberg
Vice President and OD Consulting Practice Leader, Management Performance International
Author, *Coaching Up and Down the Generations*

"If you've delivered training on the web or attended a web presentation, you will know right away that Wayne 'gets it.' This book demystifies the technology and puts the emphasis where it belongs—on your audience. Through a combination of witty humor, practical planning tools, and delivery tips, Wayne gives you permission to push your limits, experiment, learn, and even enjoy developing and delivering virtual presentations. If your goal is to engage your audience in spite of the technology, you'll find yourself using *10 Steps to Successful Virtual Presentations* as a 'go-to' career resource for a skill that is no longer optional."

> Maureen Kerr
> Manager, Instructional Design
> NACO Learning
> Weight Watchers International

"Web meetings and PowerPoint have much in common. They hold great potential but often deliver a deadly experience. *10 Steps to Successful Virtual Presentations* is your guide to avoiding the pitfalls and delivering the engaging online experience you want to create. This book is unique in addressing the specific needs of different types of web meetings from product demos to training.

In addition, the book provides job aids and templates for each step in designing and delivering a web meeting. The checklists are valuable to anyone, experienced or novice, to keep track of the actions needed for a successful session. It is a valuable asset for developing your own live online sessions as well as helping a client to develop online events."

> Christopher Saeger, CPT
> Director, Performance Improvement

10 STEPS TO

Successful
Virtual Presentations

10 STEPS TO

Successful Virtual Presentations

Wayne Turmel

ASTD PRESS
Alexandria, Virginia

ASTD Press is an internationally renowned source of insightful and practical information on workplace learning and performance topics, including training basics, evaluation and return-on-investment, instructional systems development, e-learning, leadership, and career development.

Ordering information: Books published by ASTD Press can be purchased by visiting ASTD's website at store.astd.org or by calling 800.628.2783 or 703.683.8100.

Library of Congress Control Number: 2010928320
ISBN-10: 1-56286-746-6
ISBN-13: 978-1-56286-746-1

ASTD Press Editorial Staff:
Director: Adam Chesler
Manager, ASTD Press: Jacqueline Edlund-Braun
Project Manager, Content Acquisition: Justin Brusino
Senior Associate Editor: Tora Estep
Associate Editor: Victoria DeVaux
Editorial Assistant: Stephanie Castellano
Copyeditor: Melinda Masson
Indexer: Abella Publishing Services, LLC
Interior Design and Production: Abella Publishing Services, LLC
Cover Design: Steve Fife

Printed by Versa Press, Inc., East Peoria, IL, www.versapress.com

Let's face it, most people spend their days in chaotic, fast-paced, time- and resource-strained organizations. Finding time for just one more project, assignment, or even learning opportunity—no matter how career enhancing or useful—is difficult to imagine. The *10 Steps* series is designed for today's busy professional who needs advice and guidance on a wide array of topics ranging from project management to people management, from business strategy to decision making and time management, from leading effective meetings to researching and creating a compelling presentation. Each book in this ASTD series promises to take its readers on a journey to solid understanding, with practical application the ultimate destination. This is truly a just-tell-me-what-to-do-now series. You will find action-driven language teamed with examples, worksheets, case studies, and tools to help you quickly implement the right steps and chart a path to your own success. The *10 Steps* series will appeal to a broad business audience from middle managers to upper-level management. Workplace learning and human resource professionals along with other professionals seeking to improve their value proposition in their organizations will find these books a great resource.

C O N T E N T S

P R E F A C E

After more than 15 years of teaching and coaching presentation skills, I have developed a healthy skepticism about books and advice versus practical application. I always tell my classes, "Everyone knows you shouldn't drool when you present. The real question you should be asking yourselves is, 'Can you present without drooling?'" It's the same with any behavior—theory only takes you so far.

On the surface, a book about virtual presentations makes as much sense as a book about skiing. The information might be accurate, but everything you've read flies out the window the minute you stand at the top of the hill. Looking down, you can't remember your own name, never mind how to gently turn your skis to avoid that tree that is suddenly bigger and scarier than you remember.

Here's the important distinction between web presenting and skiing—no one has ever been seriously injured (at least physically) by a web presentation gone wrong.

All of this is to say that, while a lot of good information is included in this book, much of it won't make any sense to you until you actually get your hands on whichever tool you're going to use and take it for a spin.

When I lead classes in online presenting, the one thing I hear from participants more than any other is, "I never knew all the cool stuff you can do." That's when I know I've done my job, and it's the point of this book: to show you the possibilities and lower the stress level and panic that may prevent you from trying things that bring out the best in both the tool and you, the presenter.

By all means, read this book or at least purchase it if you've come this far, but put it down periodically and log on. Push the buttons, screw things up, get bumped off, and log back on again. A book can only take you so far. At some point, you need to log on and give that first presentation.

That's what *10 Steps to Successful Virtual Presentations* is all about. Copy the tools. Use the checklists. Share the tips with your teammates and employees. Have fun. Try stuff and don't be afraid to make mistakes. Then get better and don't make that same mistake again. In no time, your presentation skills will improve, and who knows, you might even have a little fun.

INTRODUCTION

Virtual presentations. Webinars. Web demos. Synchronous online training. Another stupid web meeting. Whatever you call them, virtual presentations are part of the way people work now, and there's no going back. What's the big deal?

You might relate to these numbers:

◆ In a poll conducted for www.greatwebmeetings.com, 100 people who sat through webinar-type product demos were asked how they enjoyed them. The number-one word that showed up in written comments (about 38 of 100) was suck—not a good sign if you're a salesperson who does web presentations as part of your sales process.

◆ The vast majority of our clients who have bought web presentation licenses for their managers find that fewer than 25 percent of users feel they use the tools competently or use them at all. One client reported that fewer than 15 percent of the organization's managers actually used the tools they were given. The reasons most gave were fear of the technology and that they haven't been taught how to use it. Imagine how much money is being wasted.

◆ Seventy percent of managers in companies with more than 20 employees now have at least one team member who works remotely. More than half of managers have never received any formal training in how to manage or communicate over distance or how to build remote teams.

◆ Web conference provider WebEx estimates that more than 12 million web meetings take place each day. While no hard numbers are available for how many of those are well run and accomplish their goal, the amount of email that gets sent during the meetings suggests they're not terribly engaging or effective.

This is not to say that webinars and web meetings have to be painful for both presenter and audience. It just means that too often they are.

How to Use This Book

This book takes a macro to micro approach to becoming a web presenter. Because form should follow function, what presenters do should be based on what they're trying to achieve, who their audience is, what tools they have at their disposal, and what will get the desired outcome with those variables.

Each step will have basic information that applies to all presenters but will also break out advice specific to one of the four types of presentation (see the sidebar). For example, how you open a sales call (by asking for customer input early and not pushing your agenda) will differ from how you open a training webinar (where specific learning objectives must be explicitly stated).

This book is designed to be shared, marked up, and used. You'll find planning tools, checklists, coaching tips, and more. Reading it all at once is probably not the best plan. Pick it up, try something, and then come back. Skip to the step you need help with now, and come back to read the rest at your leisure.

Four Types of Presentations

Depending on the type of presentation you are giving, there will be a unique set of challenges and opportunities best suited to one of the four types of presentations discussed in this book:

◆ **General information webinar**. The simplest web presentations, general information webinars tend to be less interactive and often involve one speaker presenting to a large audience. They still require the basic planning and presentation skills, so these will be used for generic examples in the book.

◆ **Sales demos**. Whether you're demonstrating a complex software application or just doing a "capability presentation" for a prospect, you want to engage your audience, ask lots of questions, and move your customer through the sales cycle.

◆ **Training**. Asking members of a big audience to sit passively while you lecture or flash a bunch of PowerPoint slides at them is not training; it's data transfer. To be effective, you must use the same principles of adult learning that you would use with any other medium. The good news is that web presentations can be wonderfully effective if they're well planned and engaging in their delivery. The bad news is that many trainers who have always delivered in the classroom are uncomfortable in the new medium. If we've done our job, you'll get excited about the possibilities, and you'll be prepared to make your training really rock.

◆ **Team meetings**. A meeting that bores people, doesn't generate good discussion or quality outcomes, and leaves a bad impression of the meeting leader is worse than a waste of time. It can kill team morale and threaten your project. Saving money on air travel is no bargain if the project fails due to lack of input or the unwillingness of people to speak up and share their insights. Strong facilitation skills are key for every manager, project lead, and administrator.

Why Web Presenting Can Be Tricky

Presenting online combines two things most sane adults do not embrace enthusiastically: public speaking and technology. Everybody knows that speaking in public is the number-one fear of adults. Now imagine you have to give a speech while programming your DVR. Many people view presenting online in a similar way.

Add to this the fact that most professionals have been on the receiving end of too many bad web presentations, which has a chilling effect on their motivation to participate. Think about it: Most people would agree that a hammer is useful, but if you've never seen a hammer used correctly, you might find it hard to imagine. You might get that you can pound nails with it, for example, but not that you can also pull them out. If every web presentation you ever see is a glitch-plagued snoozefest, you won't be motivated to present, and you certainly won't want to inflict that on an innocent audience.

Also, people tend to look at web meetings and training as a weak response to a big problem. Travel costs are high, so company representatives won't travel to meet customers. Trainers are expensive, so an organization will cut the number of people in a department and have everything delivered online. Nobody wants to rush to embrace a tool that, at best, seems only to make the best of a bad situation.

Here's the good news: The problem is curable. Web presentations can be engaging, effective, and (hard as it may be to believe based on your experience so far) fun to participate in. They have innumerable possibilities. You just have to understand them and the challenges of planning and delivery.

A Success Story

Let's look at an example of how this is more than just happy talk and consultant nonsense. A large, multinational manufacturer of heavy equipment had 14 plants around the world. Each year, the plants held a Best Practices Fair, with the winner from each plant coming to Chicago to present in front of the senior leadership team. This was considered a perk for the teams—they got a free trip to Chicago and a chance to schmooze with the big dogs. They also got to network and swap ideas with dozens of their peers. Then came a budget freeze.

Suddenly, the entire project was threatened. The company couldn't afford to fly dozens of people in to present for a couple of hours. Additionally, each team member would be out of commission for a week—a loss of productivity—and the senior leaders didn't want to spend a full week sitting through endless presentations. Finally, someone suggested the idea of a "virtual" conference: Each team would get the chance to deliver its presentation online, from its facility. At least this would offer the same chance to share information while saving money.

Not surprisingly, a lot of griping ensued:

◆ The teams felt they were robbed of a reward for their hard work.

◆ They felt their work wouldn't be appreciated.

◆ The networking opportunities that would come from socializing with their peers would be lost.

◆ They wouldn't get to meet the senior leaders who could affect their careers.

As it so often is, the idea of online presentations was a grudging compromise. To be sure, it was better than not sharing the best practices at all, but no one had much hope for a successful session.

Instead of a few days crowded with PowerPoint presentations, each team got to present over 14 days. The webinars were recorded and posted on the company's intranet for everyone to see, and the winner was declared by a vote from a large group inside the company, rather than just the executives.

Much to the amazement of almost everyone, good things happened. Of course, the company saved money on travel, and the presenters didn't lose days of productive work time—everyone expected that. There were other benefits, though:

◆ Because they were recorded, the presentations were viewed by more than just a few select people. In fact, hundreds of people throughout the company viewed them.

◆ The presentations weren't presented all in one day. Each team had 14 days to conduct its presentation, so neither the intended audience nor the presenters were exhausted. They had plenty of time and energy to really absorb the information.

◆ The recorded presentations were available on the company's intranet 24/7 for a full year. This meant anyone in the company could go back and revisit the best presentations.

◆ Almost all of the ideas presented were adopted, rather than just the "winners."

◆ People throughout the company reached out across silos and locations to connect via LinkedIn, via Facebook, and on the intranet. The networking opportunities that would have come from a cocktail party actually expanded exponentially.

◆ Management spotted strong presenters and team leaders. Promotions and rewards were identical to those given to presenters in years past when they'd done "real" presentations.

Sure, a trip to the Windy City and a cocktail party would have been more fun. But if you're measuring the positive impact on the presenting teams, the company, and the shareholders, it's hard to argue with the results. In fact, in many ways, the long-term impact of the virtual conference was superior to the old way of doing things.

That's the point. Web presenting isn't better or worse than being live in front of an audience—it's just a different medium. It does some things very well (recording increases the potential audience size) and others not nearly as well (cocktail hour is just a little sad).

Target Audience

10 Steps to Successful Virtual Presentations is designed for two key audiences:

◆ Anyone who expects to find him- or herself leading a web presentation, which means almost anyone who leads teams, sells over a large territory, delivers training, or expects to have a job sometime in the 21st century. Whether you consider yourself a presenter or not, this is a key competency for most.

◆ Those brave souls who are responsible for helping organizations develop their training and learning opportunities. As you look at the functions of your organization, ask yourself, "What are the roles people are expected to fill, and how will they use web presentations?" Then identify the skill gaps, attitudes (equally important when it comes to technology adoption), and concerns that might limit successful implementation of these tools.

If you're an experienced presenter, you'll find tips to make your presentations sharper and more effective. If you're new to the medium (as are the majority of web meeting users), you'll find planning tools, checklists, and tips to make your learning curve less steep and help you relax.

The Structure of the Book

10 Steps to Successful Virtual Presentations will help you hit the ground running. You'll learn to plan, prepare for, and deliver your presentation. Here is an overview of the 10 steps:

Step 1: Identify Your Objectives and Outcomes—The first step to delivering an online presentation (or any type of presentation, really) is to understand what you are trying to accomplish. This dictates everything from your objectives to the format, style, and length of the presentation.

Step 2: Learn the Platform—Competitive analysis shows more than 100 web presentation platforms are out there. This step will help you learn whether a browser-based or non-browser-based platform is right for you, taking into account what you're trying to achieve, your experience level, and your audience. You will also learn some of the features of your type of platform and what it does well (and not so well) so you can make smart choices when putting your presentation together.

Step 3: Create a Project Plan—The biggest challenge for new web presenters is all the multitasking. By using templates and outlines, you can plan your presentation, know where the interaction takes place, and generally free up your brain to communicate with your audience. This step provides tools for effectively planning each type of presentation we'll discuss in the book (general webinars and webcasts, sales demos, training, and team meetings), which will allow you to quickly build a powerful presentation designed to be delivered online.

Step 4: Work With Others—Putting a good web presentation together requires a number of people working together. However, determining who does what, with what resources, and the appropriate material to present to an audience can help ensure a good presentation and happy stakeholders. Additionally, this step describes the so-called "joys" of presenting with another person. When is it a good idea (almost always, especially in the beginning), and how do you make it look good (a little tricky but doable)?

Step 5: Create Compelling Content—One of the biggest complaints about webinars in general is that they are not terribly interesting. You'll learn from this step how to build a presentation that keeps people's attention, adds value, achieves your objectives, and doesn't drag on.

Step 6: Create Visuals That Support Your Presentation—Webinars are a visual medium. If they weren't, you'd do a conference call and get it over with. This step will discuss what people should be looking at and provide some rules of thumb for a good web presentation.

Step 7: Sharpen Your Presentation Skills—Even people who are good presenters at the front of a room can come across as lifeless and uninteresting online. The use of *um* seems to appear out of nowhere, and, in an effort to make sure they hit all the points, presenters find themselves reading to their audience. Step 7 offers some great tips for presenting like a pro.

Step 8: Rehearse—Practicing a web meeting involves more than simply flipping through your PowerPoint deck and muttering to yourself. Troubleshoot technical problems, identify potential snags, and get comfortable with your tool before you have living, breathing people on the receiving end. No one wants to watch you learn your craft—you want to be competent, confident, and credible the minute people "meet" you online.

Step 9: Present and Multitask Effectively—If you've ever run a web meeting, you know it feels like rubbing your head, patting your tummy, and jumping up and down—while trying to give a speech. By planning, rehearsing, and just breathing deeply before presenting, you can handle the multitasking and look professional and calm under pressure.

Step 10: Follow Up and Keep Learning—Signing off your web meeting is not the end of your job. If you capture your best practices, you can avoid making the same mistakes again, help your peers learn from your experiences, and make your next presentation less stressful. You do plan to do this again, right?

Too many presenters are asked to use virtual presentation tools without understanding their full capability, their strengths, and their weaknesses. They're asked to work with tools they barely understand, yet managers are surprised that they're not confident in their use.

Let's fix that right now.

Identify Your Objectives and Outcomes

OVERVIEW

- Know your objectives
- Define your outcomes specifically
- Customize your presentation
- Make your presentation effective

Presenting online seems awfully foreign at first. No audience is available for you to connect to and draw energy from. All these buttons and tools mean you have to keep your mind on what you're doing rather than what you're saying. It can all be a bit overwhelming.

Also, you have probably been on the receiving end of less-than-riveting presentations and might think that's all there is to them. Just tell the audience what they need, and you can all get back to work. No harm, no foul, even if you know that a presentation would be so much better if you could get all of your audience members together in a room and really present to them "properly."

Of course, that describes the wrong way to look at presenting virtually, which, if done well, can be equally or more engaging than an in-person presentation. Creating an engaging virtual presentation is difficult for a number of reasons, one of which is that both presenters and audiences approach online presenting (at least at first) with trepidation, and it's easy to understand why.

Presenters aren't always comfortable moving from a face-to-face environment to the online world for a number of good reasons:

◆ Part of the fun of presenting live is connecting with people, and in a virtual presentation you're in a room by yourself.

◆ The normal rules of social etiquette you learned for live presentations don't really seem to apply. The audience for your virtual presentation can be easily distracted if they are checking their email, surfing the web, and so forth. You can't see them so they don't feel guilty about multitasking.

◆ The audience provides little or no feedback.

◆ Technology can be a distraction until you get to know it.

Research from www.greatwebmeetings.com shows audiences dread virtual presentations for three main reasons, borne out by painful past experiences:

◆ The technology is clunky.

◆ The presenters are boring.

◆ The meetings are too long and waste time.

Let's address each of these issues.

The technology is clunky. Technology will occasionally trip you up; it happens. What matters is your ability to troubleshoot and fix problems on the fly. (We will deal with that in Step 8.) If your audience isn't tech savvy or connected on a fast Internet line, then you can choose not to use features like video or webcams. Why make it hard on your audience (and yourself)?

The presenters are boring. While the feedback isn't the same as the laughter and energy you'll find in a lively meeting, you can use many tools to get good input from participants, check their buy-in, and assess their learning. A good presenter is continually checking the audience's pulse and making adjustments. As a result, a virtual presentation should never be boring—if it is, it probably has more to do with the presenter and the information presented than with the medium. Virtual presentation platforms offer numerous tools with which you can engage your audience.

The meetings are too long and waste time. The point of presenting online is not simply to present information. That's just data transfer, and you can save yourself and your audience a lot of trouble by just writing an email. Where presenters add value is by effectively communicating, listening to members of the audience, engaging them, and facilitating like a pro, which doesn't happen by accident.

That's the point of this book. By taking a methodical approach to building your web presentation, you can clear your mind of concerns, plan for things that can (and likely will) go wrong at some point, and focus on your objective.

That, of course, raises a question: What is your objective? Why are you holding a virtual meeting or webinar? What are you really trying to accomplish? This may sound basic, but it's at the core of what being a good web presenter is all about: accomplishing what you set out to do.

Know Your Objectives

Let's take a common example: You need to tell people about the new human resources benefits. We've all been to this kind of presentation—a boring PowerPoint festival with an endless amount of detail presented linearly. You basically have a checklist of things you need to tell people, and when you've told them, the presentation is over.

That fails to engage the audience and is painful (or at least dull) for the presenter. Consider what you really want to do.

Your objective is not simply telling people about the new benefits package. Your goals are to
- ◆ tell them what's different from last year
- ◆ answer as many questions as possible
- ◆ show them how to enroll
- ◆ get them excited and motivated to participate

◆ help them meet the enrollment deadline so they reap the benefits

◆ know whom to turn to for help if they need it. (If that person is you, think about how it would help if participants thought of you as competent, professional, and approachable.)

This is not a minor matter of semantics. If you just want to tell them about the benefits, the measure of success is whether or not you give them all the information. That's it. The webinar is scheduled; it is delivered (how well is really not a factor); a hundred people view it (whether they pay attention or just answer email while you drone on is irrelevant), and your work here is done.

If you have all those goals, though, your measure of success is very different. In fact, the way you structure your presentation, deliver the content, and determine success changes dramatically. What you might have there is an interesting, relevant, and effective presentation—yes, even if it's delivered online.

The term we'll use here is your objective. If you're in the training industry, you're familiar with learning objectives. A learning objective is "a statement that describes in broad terms what the learner will gain from instruction." But you don't have to be in training—every presentation of every kind should have an objective. It answers the question audience members often ask themselves: "Why am I here, and what does this have to do with me?" It meets the same criteria as a learning objective—you should be able to state clearly what the audience will take away from your time together.

Two tips for writing a good objective for your presentation follow:

◆ Be specific about what information needs to be conveyed. It will help you determine what information to include and (more important) what information can be deleted for time or saved for the question-and-answer period.

◆ Ask yourself, "So what?" An objective is only complete if you understand what members of your audience are supposed to do with the information once they have it.

Consider how this applies to the four types of presentation described in this book:

◆ **General information webinar.** At first blush, your objective might be to tell people about a policy change. That could be done in a simple email. When you ask yourself, "So what?" you discover what you really want is to give them the rationale for the change, the details, and how they can take action. You also want to answer any questions or concerns they might have in real time.

◆ **Sales demo.** Your objective is not to show people how the application works. Your objectives are to convince them that this tool will help them do whatever they need to do and to move them through the sales cycle to the next step (maybe recommending it to purchasing or even agreeing to a trial). What's your call to action going to be?

◆ **Training.** Your objective is to help the learners pick up and use a skill. Teaching them how to write good emails is only helpful if they actually then turn around and write good emails. How can you build in assessment, practice activities, and coaching to make this true training?

◆ **Team meeting.** Your objective could be to brainstorm solutions to a problem. If that's the case, you should start thinking about ways to encourage participation. How many people should be in that meeting? What are their roles? How will they interact?

POINTER

If your objective is to tell someone about a topic, you probably haven't defined your objective clearly enough. The next question you need to ask yourself is, "So what?"

Define Your Outcomes Specifically

Now that you know what you want to accomplish as the presenter, you need to think about your audience. Ask yourself: What do you want audience members to do with the information once they have it? For example, if you want them to start filling out their timesheets in a certain way, then that's the desired outcome. If your audience is the sales team, you don't want them to just "know the product," you want them to get out there and schedule appointments with their customers to talk about it. We'll get into more specific details on this topic in Step 2.

Getting your point across will determine the success of your presentation.

Consider this: "When my presentation is over, I want my audience to _____ as a result."

How would you fill in that blank? You want that information to be specific, action oriented, and realistic. If you're giving a project status update, you want your audience to understand the current state of the project (good news, bad news), and you must be very clear about next steps, what needs to happen, by when, and by whom.

Both you and your audience must understand the purpose clearly before you even begin to create your presentation. Ask yourself why this information matters to you and why it should matter to your audience.

Why It Matters to You

◆ This will guide you in choosing the content and tools you're going to use.
◆ People have short attention spans. Focus on the content that's critical to achieving your outcomes so your presentation isn't too long or bloated.
◆ When you ask yourself, "Why am I doing this?" you can answer the question.

Why It Matters to Your Audience

◆ A person's ability to focus is directly related to his or her interest in the topic. To get people focused immediately, you must give them a clear reason for paying attention.

◆ If you want members of your audience to do something, you need to clearly express it. If you've ever sat through a presentation and wondered, "OK, now what?" you know how important that is.

POINTER

You should be able to write out the outcome in a single sentence, but no more than two.

Identify the Challenges to Achieving Your Goals

Now that you know what you want to accomplish, and what you want your audience to do when the presentation is over, you may feel you're ready to present.

Not so fast. No matter how clear, well designed, or brilliantly delivered your presentation is, you'll only achieve your outcomes if the audience is able and willing to receive the message and then take the action you urge.

Plenty of barriers prevent that understanding. Presenting on-line is different from presenting in person for a number of reasons, and this makes it tough for both you and your audience. By identifying any challenges before you start to build your presentation, you can mitigate or overcome them. If all else fails, you'll be prepared if something does go wrong.

For the presenter, some of the barriers include

◆ too much information that can either confuse or bore your audience (In cyberspace, you can't see the glazed or panicked looks on participants' faces.)

◆ frustration because participants are experiencing difficulty connecting to the presentation or having audio trouble

◆ lack of interaction, making it feel like you're presenting into the void

◆ difficulty multitasking, which makes it hard to concentrate.

For the participants, barriers include

◆ connection or audio problems

◆ discomfort with communicating through this medium

◆ reluctance to ask the questions they should ask

◆ busy schedules and distracting tasks like email

◆ other distractions like whatever is going on at the next cube

◆ the presenter going too fast for the audience to ask questions

◆ looking at a computer screen passively, which makes it hard for even the most motivated professionals to stay engaged for very long

◆ language or cultural barriers

◆ little or no experience with the topic of the presentation.

The good news is that most of these problems can be lessened (if not completely eliminated) with some planning and forethought. That's why understanding your audience is so critical. To help you understand your audience, review the Audience Analysis Checklist (Worksheet 1.1), which includes many of the things a good presenter should know about his or her audience, but also includes things specific to the online world. Asking members of your audience whether they have ever been to a web meeting is helpful because, if you are expecting the audience to use polling or the chat feature, you have to be sure they know how to use those tools. Don't assume that your audience is any more comfortable being a virtual audience than you are being a virtual presenter.

For example, at a major nonprofit relief agency, a big barrier to web meeting effectiveness was that the majority of the audience was made up of retired volunteers. These folks were not particularly computer-savvy—they didn't spend their lives texting, sending instant messages, and sitting through web meetings, so they were largely passive observers. By simply taking a few minutes at the beginning of their webinars to have people try to send messages, the presenters greatly increased the amount of interaction, feedback, and audience satisfaction.

Step 5 looks at ways to do this, but for now let's just consider the audience in general.

Customize Your Presentation

Different presentations have different projected outcomes, so it only makes sense that they have factors unique to them. An all-hands meeting, for example, would have a broad audience and a modest outcome, while a sales meeting would be aimed at a very specific and small audience with a very specific (and high-stakes) outcome.

Consider the following nuances, depending on the presentation you're planning:

General webinars. How many people are you planning to have attend? Will you want to take questions by voice or have participants ask the questions via chat or a question-and-answer box?

Sales demos. What do people know already about your presentation or service? What are the top two or three questions they need answered to move you through the sales process? Who else will be involved in the decision? What objections will you have to overcome?

Training. Do you know people's current level of interest in the subject? What about their skill level? How will you test or assess

POINTER

If you are not familiar with the audience or don't know the answers to some of these questions before you start presenting, plan to use some of the interactive tools at your disposal (such as the chat feature). Plan to get as much information as you can before you go too far down the road. Polling is a great way to find out your audience's experience level or attitude about your subject—the equivalent of the icebreaker you would use in a regular face-to-face meeting.

them after the training? Is there work you can assign before or afterward that will help you measure your success and reduce the time you need to spend online?

Team meetings. How much interaction will you want? Is your role to deliver information or to facilitate conversation and get the most out of your team? When was the last time the team got together—would a webcam be helpful?

Make Your Presentation Effective

As a presenter in a face-to-face situation, you can do lots of things to make a presentation more interactive and engaging, such as asking participants to raise their hands, allowing them to ask questions as they occur (rather than waiting until the end), and asking them questions to gauge their knowledge and attitude. While the mechanics of these activities are a little different in a virtual presentation, a lot of similarities exist.

In any presentation, you want to do the following:

◆ **Ask questions.** Asking effective questions is a great way to keep audience members engaged and interested. It also lets you know how much detail you have to go into so you don't bore them.

◆ **Capture best practices and suggestions just as you would on a flipchart or whiteboard.** By letting audience members participate, you are not just transferring information but allowing them to share wisdom with each other. It changes the dynamic of the meeting from a passive experience to an active one.

◆ **Create human connections with the use of your visuals.** Details will be provided in a later step, but people want to hear from people, not machines. If they can see your smiling face, they'll be more inclined to pay attention and take the action you want them to take.

◆ **Conduct small group work if possible, but note that this takes some skill to pull off.** When you learn the tools (and, trust me, you will), you'll find ways to replicate many classroom activities. Helping the group members come to their own conclusions rather than simply telling them what to think aids buy-in and moves them closer to the action you want them to take—and they'll think they had the idea.

◆ **Brainstorm and collaborate.** In many ways, online collaboration works better because you can space it out over time. By combining online and offline (synchronous and asynchronous) tools, you can avoid groupthink, get the best out of everyone, and make better decisions.

There's no excuse for making virtual presentations boring, static, or unproductive.

Wrap-Up

Online presenting is not radically different from any other presentation you'll ever do—it just has some unique wrinkles. The basics remain:

◆ Understand your objectives.

◆ Decide which actions will determine success.

◆ Take the time to consider your audience members and what it will take to move them to do whatever it is you need them to do with your information.

◆ Start with what you would do in a perfect world to achieve your objectives, and then take a good look at your tools to decide how close you can come to creating those conditions.

Now that you know what you want to accomplish, it's time to face the "elephant in the room" and the reason presenting online stresses most people out: the technology.

Audience Analysis Checklist

Before you charge off and start building your presentation, take some time to check your assumptions about your audience. Sit down with this chart and ask yourself the following questions.

In the section marked "What You Do Know," put only those things that you know for a fact are true. If you are guessing, be honest with yourself. Sometimes you have to go on a hunch, but the more you know for sure, the better.

Some sample answers to "Why It's Important" are included to guide your thinking. The simplest way to think of these is, "So, what does this mean to me for making my presentation as successful as possible?"

Audience Analysis

What You Should Know	What You Do Know	Why It's Important
How many people will be at the web meeting?		In general, the more people attending a meeting, the less interactive it will be.
Have they attended a web meeting before?		Will they be comfortable participating?
Will everyone be online, or will some people be together physically?		If some people are in a conference room sharing a speakerphone, interaction via chat will be limited. You may also have a lot of background noise, and facilitating a question-and-answer period could take some coordination.
How will they connect (broadband, dial-up)?		Connecting through slow connections means that video, webcam, and some other functions will run slower and even freeze completely.
Are the audio and video connected?		If both audio and video are over the web, participants can listen on their computers through speakers or headphones and participate with microphones. If audio and video are separate and something happens to the webinar video, participants can still listen in on the microphone even if they can't see.

What You Should Know	What You Do Know	Why It's Important
What is their level of expertise with your subject?		If participants are experienced and knowledgeable, don't bore them with background; get to the point. If they aren't, you might need some good solid examples of what you're talking about to help them understand the context.
Do they know the background of the meeting or presentation?		Have people asked for more information on your topic? Were they told what to expect or just to show up? This affects their mindset and willingness to engage with your topic.
Do they understand the primary objective and outcomes of the meeting?		If not, then it should be part of the introduction so they pay attention.
Have they received an agenda in advance?		How can they be prepared to participate and be in the right mindset if they don't know what's being discussed? Can you get an agenda to them before your presentation starts?
Do they want to be at this meeting? Why or why not?		How can you make it worth their while?
What are their roles: Are they decision makers, influencers, or implementers?		If you're asking people to make a decision, they must have the authority to do so. If your goal is to encourage them to take action, do you know what action they can actually take?
What external factors might interfere with their concentration?		Is attending your presentation the last thing they'll do before they leave for the day? That can affect concentration. Will they be in home offices? Cubicles? If they're at work, get them to turn off their email and other distractions.
If you were an attendee, what would be the single most important takeaway message from the meeting or presentation?		If you can't answer this question, you're not ready to start. If you can, do you have the visuals to help people retain your key points?

STEP 1

STEP 1

What You Should Know	What You Do Know	Why It's Important
Are there time zones or language barriers to consider?		If language is a problem, make sure to speak slowly and have plenty of text on the slides to reinforce your points—many people read a language better than they speak or translate it. Also, if it's the middle of the night, apologize for keeping people up—it is only polite and helps build rapport.
Are they internal to your organization or outsiders?		Terminology, jargon, and acronyms might cause confusion; plus you might have to introduce yourself or your company as part of the presentation.

N O T E S

_____

_____

_____

_____

_____

_____

_____

_____

_____

_____

_____

Learn the Platform

OVERVIEW

> Learn why technology causes stress

> Understand web presentation platform types

> Understand web presentation platform features

> Use the platform's features and tools for maximum impact

Odds are this step is the reason you purchased this book. After all, if you're an experienced presenter, you're probably good at many of the presentation aspects, and it's the technology that's throwing you for a loop. Conversely, if you are not a great presenter but have to present online anyway, the tools are likely still the part you care most about because they make up the largest unknown factor. Nerves you're already familiar with—technology is just an additional challenge.

Do not look at technology as a necessary evil. First, you'll never get comfortable with something you use grudgingly and as infrequently as possible. Second, when you focus on what you don't like about something, you fail to see the possibilities, and these are what is most important for you to take away from this book: the possibilities and the many ways these tools can expand your reach and achieve your objectives.

Look at the potential the technology allows:

◆ You can reach an unlimited number of people. (However, just because you can have a couple of hundred people on a webcast doesn't necessarily mean you should.)

◆ A live presentation only reaches the people in the room at that moment. Online presentations can live on after the event and reach a broader audience. Almost any online presentation can be recorded and posted for later reference. From my clients' experience, as well as from platform providers (such as BrightTALK), it is expected that four to 10 times more people will view the recorded event than will see the live presentation.

◆ You can reach people anywhere at any time.

◆ No travel costs are incurred, and less time away from work is required.

With all the benefits of web presentations, it is a wonder more people don't embrace them.

Why Technology Causes Stress

Even the most calm and rational human beings are driven by emotions and factors that don't make sense on paper. Reluctance to adopt virtual presentation tools is no different.

Old-fashioned stage fright stems from the way people were hardwired early in their evolution: If you feel a set of eyes on you, be prepared to run or fight because something might want to make you its lunch. The amygdala fires, the adrenaline and cortisol flow, and you're on red alert. The same biological turmoil occurs when you stand up to give a presentation to your boss, even though the odds of being killed and eaten are remote (actual consumption is extremely rare).

So anytime you present, you're already stressed and nervous. Technology adds another level of stress to the mix:

◆ You feel like you have no control over whether or not the platform will crash, people's computers will freeze, or the audio connection will drop for no reason.

◆ You have to remember to speak at the same time you're searching the screen for which button to push. (If you don't think that kind of multitasking is tough, think of all the times you were driving and had to turn down the car radio while looking for an address.)

◆ It can be difficult to gauge audience reaction. You're essentially presenting into what feels like a void. Without feedback it's very easy to panic and speed up, imagining a negative reaction that's not there.

◆ Odds are good that you've never seen a well-run web presentation, so you assume the audience is having the same reaction to this event that you would have.

The focus here is not to frighten you but to emphasize the importance of acknowledging what's going on so you can address it. When you know why something is stressful, it allows you to do two things:

◆ Recognize what's happening so that it doesn't catch you by surprise. You can respond appropriately.

◆ Address potential problems that you are worried about and, more important, get familiar with the tool so that your stress level is reduced. When you feel relaxed, you can concentrate on what you're trying to communicate. Practice reduces uncertainty.

Many people are familiar with the "conscious competence" model, but it bears repeating here (see Figure 2.1). According to psychologist W. S. Howell (and many others since), people go through four stages when they learn anything new:

◆ **Unconscious Incompetence**: You don't know something, but you don't know that you don't know—so it doesn't matter. What you're doing works just fine, in your opinion.

◆ **Conscious Incompetence**: You are aware that you don't know how to do something. Resistance to change kicks in. Where once you were perfectly comfortable (or at least functional), you now are not nearly as good at the job as you were before. Your internal critic works overtime, and you feel overwhelmed and defensive. This is where the "this is stupid and I hate it" feeling kicks in.

- **Conscious Competence**: After a lot of practice, you can do what's expected of you, even if you have to work at it. For web presenters, this means being at least as comfortable online as in front of a live audience. You might not love it, but you're fully functional.

- **Unconscious Competence**: You don't even have to think about what you're doing, an attainment seldom reached by presenters. Your nerves are at a minimum, you are comfortable with your content, and the technology holds no surprises for you. You feel totally "in the moment" and are having a great time.

FIGURE 2.1

Conscious Competence Model

Here's how the "conscious competence model" plays out with web presenters. You can see how the notion of conscious competence can undermine even the confidence of good presenters—maybe especially so. Embrace the chaos and know with practice and familiarity you too may become unconsciously competent.

Unconscious Incompetence	Conscious Incompetence
You have never presented at a web meeting.	You have seen things go wrong with web meetings.
You have never seen a web meeting.	You have never used the tool but are willing to try.
You have avoided web meetings at all costs.	You have used the tool, but it went horribly awry.
	You hate technology.
	You are a nervous wreck.

Conscious Competence	Unconscious Competence
You have used the technology a couple of times.	You can use the tool without too much stress.
You have tried and can use the various features.	You actually have grown to like it.
You are not necessarily comfortable using the technology.	You are willing to try new features of the tool.
Just because you can use a particular tool doesn't mean you like it (yet).	You might be getting a bit cocky about your expertise in this area of technology.

Before trying to learn the platform yourself, participate in as many webinars and online presentations as possible (there's no shortage of free presentations out there). See what good presenters do (which you'll want to emulate) and how poor presenters fumble (so you never perform the same way in front of any audience). Notice all the different tools and functions other presenters use, and imagine how they can help you in your presentations.

When you get frustrated (and you will), cut yourself some slack. Really good, comfortable, traditional presenters often struggle the most with virtual presenting: They have the most to lose and are unaccustomed to feeling panic and uncertainty when they speak. After all, not many people would voluntarily feel insecure, unprofessional, and out of control if they could help it.

Accept that you will feel uncomfortable and insecure at first. It's part of the learning process.

Web Presentation Platform Types

A discussion of all web presentation software would be impossible; more than 100 different packages are out there, with more added all the time. As if that weren't daunting enough, most of them do version or feature upgrades at least once a year. If this book tried to go platform by platform or feature by feature, it would be out of date before it got to you.

In this book, we're not teaching you to use any particular platform. We'll show you a couple of different screen views from WebEx and Dimdim, so you can focus on functionality (see Figure 2.2 and Figure 2.3 on page 25). These views are what the presenter would see on a standard WebEx or Dimdim screen. Don't be intimidated. We will walk you through the tools and you'll master the skills in no time.

Consider the two general categories of web presenting platforms: browser based and non-browser based. The specific technical details are kept to a minimum; what follows is only what you really need to know.

The good news is that covering all platforms isn't necessary because most perform the same functions. If you become proficient in one, you can transfer your skills to another with a minimal amount of adjustment.

Browser-Based Applications

Browser-based applications run from your desktop—what's on your computer is what your audience sees. These platforms include GoToMeeting, VIA3, and Glance. Among the advantages are the following:

◆ PowerPoint animation will probably work smoother and better than with uploadable platforms.

◆ Lag time for application sharing is usually less.

◆ The fact that neither the presenter nor the audience needs to download anything tends to be appreciated by information-technology (IT) professionals who are worried about people loading unauthorized software onto their computers.

◆ It's easier to set up meetings on the fly. "Down and dirty" is usually sufficient for team meetings, sales demos, and other meetings where speed and convenience are important.

A disadvantage of this type of platform is lack of security. You are essentially sharing your computer with others, so you should be aware of those with whom you're meeting in a virtual context.

Server-Based Applications

Server-based applications require you to upload your presentation or information to a central server, and it goes out to the audience from there. This category includes most of the well-known platforms, for example WebEx, Microsoft Live Meeting, and Adobe Connect, and others such as iLinc and Dimdim. The advantages of these types of platforms are as follows:

- They tend to be sold as company-wide, enterprise solutions, so there's consistency in who's using what platform across the whole organization.
- In general, they are very stable. Because everything is sent out from the platform provider, you are less at the mercy of your computer equipment.
- They are (in general) more feature-rich than other platforms and have more interactive tools, such as chat, polling, and webcams.

A couple of disadvantages are that animation tends not to work as well as on other platforms, and, while application sharing works well, there's a chance of longer lag time (these platforms send a lot more code through the web to the audience, and this can be a problem for people with slow Internet connections).

A final note: There used to be a major division between platforms that were browser based and those that required download. In the latest versions, however, most downloadable platforms have browser-based versions. For more information, check out a comparison site like Robin Good's comparison at www.masternewmedia.org.

POINTER Roughly speaking, 90 percent of the platforms perform 90 percent of the same functions.

Web Presentation Platform Features

Once you learn some of the main features of a web presentation platform, you will be able to apply that knowledge to any other platform. Here are nine main features that you need to learn:

- audio
- PowerPoint and document sharing
- application and desktop sharing

◆ whiteboards
◆ chat
◆ polling
◆ annotation tools
◆ recording
◆ webcams and video.

Reviewing the Web Platform Comparison Checklist (Worksheet 2.1) at the end of Step 2 might be a good place to start.

Audio

The most important part of a web presentation may be the audio. Basically there are two ways to get audio for your web presentation:
◆ the telephone
◆ Voice over Internet Protocol (VoIP).

Guidelines for Telephone Usage

◆ Use a landline phone rather than a cell phone for presenting. The quality is significantly better and more reliable.
◆ Use a headset if possible. You want your hands free to run your presentation tools and to gesture and project physical energy. It's hard to sound excited with your head tilted and your phone tucked in the crook of your neck.
◆ If you can't use a headset, a speakerphone will work, but be aware that you will pick up all the background noise in your presentation space.
◆ If members of your audience are going to use the telephone rather than the audio provided by the platform provider, make sure they know how to mute their phones. The more people are on the call, the more any background noise will intrude and degrade your own sound.
◆ There is a difference between "mute" and "hold." A lot of web presentations and meetings have been ruined because someone put his or her phone on hold and all everyone heard was a chorus of beeping or unpleasant muzak.

STEP **2**

- Many companies control telephony costs by using their regular audio conferencing provider for all web meetings and presentations. This is fine. In fact, it is often superior because the host of the call can control who is allowed to speak and when it is appropriate to mute all callers.
- If you have more than six people on a call, consider muting all callers until you want them to speak. This minimizes the odds of distractions and background noise interfering.

Guidelines for Voice over Internet Protocol (VoIP)

- You need a microphone and a headset.
- Turn off your computer's speakers. Leaving them on and using the microphone in your computer will give you unpleasant feedback and cause significant delays.
- If you plan to open the microphones for the audience members to participate, make sure they know to use headsets and microphones instead of the microphone in their webcam or laptop. This information should be provided in bold letters in the invitation to the meeting.
- If you're a presenter, you don't need to spend a lot of money on a microphone, but don't buy a cheap one either. A good headset/microphone combination will run you about $40–$50. This is a much cheaper solution than using the phone lines, especially internationally.
- You are at the mercy of the speed of people's Internet connection. This type of presentation will work best if you know everyone in your audience has a broadband connection.

The key to effective audio is to keep your pace crisp and energetic, but not too fast. Refer to Step 9 on presenting effectively for ways to do that.

Remember that audio can (and, whenever possible, should) be a two-way tool. Encourage people to participate by asking for feedback in specific situations such as a question-and-answer period.

As the presenter, it's your job to facilitate and direct traffic so you won't be interrupted unnecessarily, but people should feel comfortable contributing.

PowerPoint and Document Sharing

This is the most basic feature and the one that most people identify with web presentations. The core of most virtual presentations is a slide show deck that you share with the audience, but you can share any document you create, for example, PDF files or text documents, which can make true collaboration possible. Imagine members of your team seeing you create and make changes to the team charter as you go. Or imagine showing your team how you created the annual budget, taking suggestions as you go.

If you are using animation in your slides, be aware that it may function a little differently in this environment. Be sure to test any animated slides before your presentation to ensure they work the way you intended.

Application and Desktop Sharing

This allows you to share any type of application on your computer. Imagine you're doing a sales call or conducting a training seminar for a particular technical tool and you want people to experience the product live, in real time. Not only can you show participants the product, but you can also actually let them input data and experience the software for themselves.

POINTER

When demonstrating a computer application or training people in its use, one of the most powerful things you can do is let them use the tool themselves. To do this, you need to give an audience member "presenter" status. Many presentation platforms allow you to change the presenter at any given time. WebEx, for example, allows you to pass a little "ball" icon to a new presenter by simply right-clicking on a person's name and hitting the "make presenter" button. On other platforms you can right-click on a person's name and make him or her the presenter.

FIGURE 2.2

Standard User Interface (Presenter View)

Source: This screenshot has been reproduced by ASTD Press with the permission of Cisco Systems Inc. and/or its affiliated entities. © 2010 Cisco Systems, Inc. and/or its affiliated entities. All rights reserved. Cisco and the Cisco logo are trademarks or registered trademarks of Cisco and/or its affiliates in the United States and other countries. A listing of Cisco's trademarks can be found at www.cisco.com/go/trademarks

FIGURE 2.3

Standard User Interface (Presenter View) Dimdim

Source: Photo courtesy of Dimdim.

Application and desktop sharing is one of the most powerful tools at your disposal and the one most presenters fear using. As with any of these tools, rehearse using it before your actual presentation.

Whiteboards

If you're an experienced trainer or meeting facilitator, you have probably consumed a great deal of paper by using flip charts. They're wonderful tools: You can use them for brainstorming, creating lists, giving instructions, and even taking issues offline in "the parking lot." The whiteboard on many platforms gives you the same ability without the environmental consequences. Simply share the whiteboard with your audience and write on it using the text tool.

Some platforms allow you to cut and paste pictures or text directly, but that's an advanced skill that most platforms don't do well. You should know that this tool is prone to lag, so often as much as a minute will pass between the time you type something on the whiteboard and the time it appears on your audience's screens.

An advantage to this tool is many platforms allow you to save the whiteboard as a Word document so that you have a permanent record of your activities. This is great for team meetings, taking minutes, and other functions.

Chat

This tool allows you to come close to the interaction you would experience in a live meeting. It also intimidates many new presenters because they fear losing control of the meeting, and it adds to their stress because they have to follow what's going on in the chat while they're presenting.

The power of using the chat function cannot be stressed enough, especially if you have a large number of participants and want to engage them. Here's the best way to think about it. During a live presentation, some conversation among audience members isn't always a bad thing. That's where you get questions; participants give their own examples and generate energy. There are even laughs to be had. Yes, it can be disruptive, and it's up to you as the presenter to set the ground rules and facilitate the meeting effectively so things don't get out of hand. It is the exact same thing with online presentations.

The following are four occasions when you would want to encourage people to chat:

◆ You want them to be interested right from the beginning. By encouraging them to chat, you send a clear signal you don't want them to just put you on mute and answer email—you expect them to participate.

◆ You want to lessen their trepidation about using technology.

◆ You want to assess their knowledge without conducting formal polls and assessments—a simple "true or false" or "agree or disagree" question is a great way to make sure you're on point and they're following along.

◆ You want them to know each other. In team meetings, they will be a stronger unit for knowing the strengths and weaknesses of other members. Allow them to add input, make comments, or question the speaker.

You have a lot of power as the presenter. If you want participants' input but don't want them chatting with each other, you can use the participant or attendee permissions feature. You can allow them to chat with each other in the public room (where everyone can see everything), send chat messages only to the speaker, or chat with each other privately.

Chat is probably where you'll find the biggest technology gap with your audience.

Younger audiences, who spend a lot of time texting each other and chatting on Facebook or instant messaging, will know instinctively how to use the tool, and you probably couldn't stop them if you tried. Less tech-savvy audience members might not be as familiar with the tool. They may not know that LOL is a compliment (it means "laughing out loud") or feel comfortable typing their thoughts. A little patience and encouragement will get them involved.

Polling

This tool allows you to ask questions of your audience and get the answers in a form that is easy to share. You can ask a multiple-choice question such as, "What department are you with?" and see the results as percentages of the audience. Or you can administer quick assessments and quizzes. This is a fairly sophisticated feature and is best used with larger audiences where just asking questions out loud won't let you hear from everyone.

Polling is a good tool for engaging the audience early—it's actually fun to vote and see the answers appear. Audience members won't feel quite so isolated and will have a chance to participate rather than sit passively. This tool also allows you to see the data as colorful graphs, which is a great way to make your presentation more visually arresting.

Depending on the platform, you can either build these polls and questions well in advance of your presentation or log in to your presentation early and have them ready to go.

More sophisticated applications like Cisco WebEx Training Center and Citrix GoToTraining allow you to see individual answers to questions (good for training, but you probably don't want to share such information with your audience) and keep transcripts so you can use the data after the event.

Figure 2.4 is a screen shot of Cisco's WebEx Training Center. Notice that it has a slightly different look than on the standard screen (Figure 2.2), but the basic functions are the same. Think of

FIGURE 2.4

Cisco WebEx Training Center

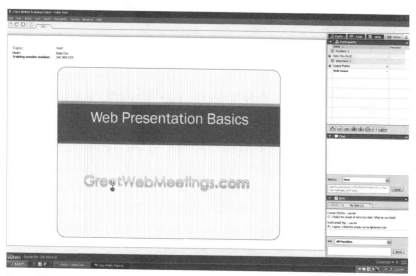

it as getting in a rental car. It might be different than the car you have at home, but with a little care you can operate the rental just fine.

Annotation Tools

One of the simplest ways to liven up the visuals in your presentation is to use what are often referred to as annotation tools. These include highlighters, which allow you to mark up your PowerPoint slides for emphasis; text tools, so you can write on the slides for brainstorming; and various colorful pointers, check marks, and arrows so you can check off the bullet points as you cover them, point out visual data, and generally give people something interesting to look at.

More than a minute or two looking at the same PowerPoint slide will make even the most dedicated audience member start to tune out. Learning to speak in front of a group while adding visual excitement to your computer screen is a great way to build your credibility as a presenter, generate audience interest, and stay engaged as a presenter.

You can also allow participants to use annotation tools to write on a whiteboard, mark up a PowerPoint slide, or show you, for example, where they think the new swimming pool should go on your design.

Remember to ensure your permissions settings are configured to your specifications. This way, you can avoid such distractions as someone mysteriously doodling on the screen because he or she wants to know what that button does. Double check your permissions settings and tell your audience members in what ways and when they can mark up the screen.

POINTER

Don't try to circle things with your mouse using the highlighter tool—it's too difficult. Most platforms have a circle tool (and a box tool) that will create perfect circles around what you're trying to highlight. With a little practice, you'll be able to place the tool perfectly and, with a drag and click of the mouse, draw a perfect circle (or rectangle).

Recording

One of the great advantages of a webinar or virtual presentation over an in-person presentation is that creating a permanent record of the event is incredibly easy. There are numerous ways for a webinar to be useful. For example, a webinar can be a training tool to bring new people up to speed. As a meeting tool, it can allow people who couldn't attend the event to view the record of what happened (no more excuses for missing action items!). It can also be a coaching tool for you as a presenter. You can view your presentation as a means of improvement.

Think about what this means for team meetings. No longer will those who aren't able to participate have to rely on meeting minutes or secondhand reports. If people can't attend your event, they will be able to go back and view it at their leisure. Training becomes more than an event—people can access your knowledge on demand. This is a great example of how recorded presentations can have greater reach than traditional presentations.

POINTER
The no-show rate for a free marketing webinar is about 50 percent. You exponentially increase your viewership by making your webinar recording available after the live event.

Plan to record your web presentations for later use. Most platforms make it easy to save recorded web presentations in a shared file or even embed them on websites for archiving. Recording also makes a great training and coaching tool. You can review your recorded sessions and see what the audience sees and hears. Sometimes it can be painful, but there's no better feedback mechanism for presenters.

The best part is that if you're unhappy with the results or you do the presentation again and get a better version, recordings are easy to delete.

POINTER
If you're going to save the recordings for posting to a website later, make sure that your provider allows you to save them in a format that is easily edited. AVI or WMV files are easier to work with than Adobe Flash. Flash is great if you want to post a whole recording or use something like SlideShare or Brainshark, which are online resources that allow you to capture PowerPoint presentations and even add voice narration to them. If you're adventurous, you may prefer to edit your recordings in Camtasia or another editing software, add music and titles, and make them look great. It's difficult for the average person to do this in Flash.

Webcams and Video

These tools hold a lot of promise but are the source of much frustration for both audience members and presenters. They do some things very well (create human connections) and have their difficulties (tend to freeze up). Just know that unless both you as the presenter and your audience have good, high-speed Internet connections, you are setting yourself up for a rough experience with video freezing and computers crashing.

A good way to use your webcam is to turn it on during the beginning of your presentation to create a connection with your audience and then turn it off after introductions.

Showing streaming video during a webinar or web presentation is still difficult. Short clips work best, but make sure you test them thoroughly on a variety of computers and with various levels of Internet connection before making them a critical part of your presentation.

Use these tools where appropriate, but until the technology catches up with demand, use them sparingly.

> **POINTER** A great way to create human connections but not make yourself crazy is to use your webcam to introduce yourself to the audience and then turn it off when you begin the body of your presentation. This will save bandwidth (reducing the chance of something freezing up for you or your audience) and also free you from worrying about what you look like while presenting. In cyberspace, no one needs to see you scratch your nose.

Using the Platform's Features and Tools for Maximum Impact

Having these tools at your disposal doesn't mean you have to use all of them, every time. What it means is that by carefully considering what you're trying to accomplish, you can make smart choices about what to use.

Consider the following four types of web presentation and how their various functions could be used strategically to get where you want to go.

General Webinars

These presentations are usually one-to-many broadcasts, which means you have a large audience that you want to keep engaged while you get your message across. To do this, you might want to use one of the following tools:

◆ Internet audio—this means they'll be listening and speaking through their computer speakers, microphone, or headset. This is becoming more common as the technology improves and more people use laptops with built-in cameras and speakers. It's cheaper for large audiences, and they won't need to speak anyway. Many platforms, like the "GoTo" family of products actually allow you to have a mix of telephone and Internet audio.

◆ Webcam—because not everyone at the meeting will know who you are, you want to connect with participants as best as you can.

◆ Polling—before launching into your presentation, you might want to know what audience members' level of knowledge or comfort is with the topic. If geographical information is important, polling is a great tool for finding out that information.

◆ Chat—encourage comments and examples from the audience as you go along. Don't hold questions until the end, when it's too late to adjust your presentation.

◆ Annotation tools—use the highlighter and check features if you're going to be on a single screen for a long time.

◆ Recording—post the webinar later for those who missed it the first time.

Sales Demos

These tend to be one-on-one or small group meetings, so you have the opportunity to provide more individual attention and build a connection. These are some tools that work well for this type of presentation:

◆ Audio—make it as simple as possible for audience members to connect and speak. You want them asking questions and speaking just as they would on a real sales call.

◆ Webcam—if possible, have the audience on a webcam as well. Many platforms allow for two-way video.

◆ Share applications—let the prospect play with the tool. If it's as intuitive as you say, let participants feel it for themselves.

Training

All good training follows adult learning methodologies. Engaging the audience frequently is important. Think about what you would do in the classroom and consider these tools:

◆ Polling—assess your audience's knowledge and attitude. What do members know about the subject already? How do they feel about it? You can design pre- and postsession quizzes.

◆ Chat—let audience members submit questions in writing and by voice. Allow them to talk among themselves in private and in public.

◆ Annotation tools—use highlighters, arrows, and the circle tool to help people remember key points and words.

Team Meetings

To get the most input from the audience, you will want to use a combination of tools:

◆ Audio—if the meeting is small, keep the phone lines open (ask audience members to mute their phones if there is background noise where they are).

- Webcam and video—help attendees see each other. If your platform allows multiple webcams, have each person turn on his or her webcam while introducing him- or herself to the group and then turn it off. You can also have attendees do this when asking questions.
- Whiteboard—keep a running list of action items and topics for further discussion.
- Application and desktop sharing—when working on documents as a team, actually work on the live document. Audience members find this much more engaging, and they'll see their input being used immediately.

Wrap-Up

Your goal is to communicate exactly the right amount of information to make your point. Understanding your web conferencing platform and mastering its available tools are vital to that process. Take these next steps:

- Determine which platform you will use (your organization may have already decided this for you).
- Understand what features are available to you.
- Participate in other webcasts to see what other presenters do well.
- Practice with your specific platform and get comfortable with its tools and features.

You can make the right call about what tools to use to achieve your goal. Furthermore, you'll know you can use them effectively when the time comes.

WORKSHEET 2.1

Web Platform Comparison Checklist

Here are some of the most commonly requested features for choosing a web presentation platform.

To use this chart:

- ◆ Select the features that are going to be most useful or important to you in achieving your goals.
- ◆ Prioritize them in order of importance to you and your outcomes.

Feature	Yes/No	Comments
Download required	Y ☐ N ☐	
Fully Macintosh useful	Y ☐ N ☐	
Fully PC useful	Y ☐ N ☐	
Live video/webcam	Y ☐ N ☐	
Video for both presenter/audience	Y ☐ N ☐	
Streaming video clips	Y ☐ N ☐	
Slides/PowerPoint	Y ☐ N ☐	
Full PowerPoint animation	Y ☐ N ☐	
Thumbnail/slide manipulation during event	Y ☐ N ☐	
Application sharing	Y ☐ N ☐	
Desktop sharing	Y ☐ N ☐	
Annotation tools	Y ☐ N ☐	
Web sharing	Y ☐ N ☐	
Chat	Y ☐ N ☐	
Both public and private chat	Y ☐ N ☐	
Saves chat logs	Y ☐ N ☐	
Separate Q&A function	Y ☐ N ☐	
Whiteboard	Y ☐ N ☐	
Cut and paste to whiteboard	Y ☐ N ☐	
Multiple presenter controls	Y ☐ N ☐	
Polling	Y ☐ N ☐	
Multiple format polling (true or false, multiple choice, multiple answer)	Y ☐ N ☐	
Audience feedback tools	Y ☐ N ☐	
Attention monitoring	Y ☐ N ☐	
LMS integration	Y ☐ N ☐	

Worksheet 2.1, continued

Feature	Yes/No	Comments
Collaboration tools/workgroups	Y ❑ N ❑	
On-air breakout groups	Y ❑ N ❑	
Works across networks and platforms	Y ❑ N ❑	
Email integration	Y ❑ N ❑	
Automated thank-you/confirm letters	Y ❑ N ❑	
Registration function	Y ❑ N ❑	
Calendar function	Y ❑ N ❑	
E-commerce for registration or subscription	Y ❑ N ❑	
System check	Y ❑ N ❑	
On-air moderator assistance	Y ❑ N ❑	
Tech support during event	Y ❑ N ❑	
Customer-branded interface	Y ❑ N ❑	
Customized landing page	Y ❑ N ❑	
Live presenter training	Y ❑ N ❑	
Online tutorials/demos	Y ❑ N ❑	
Project management/coaching services	Y ❑ N ❑	
Records: audio/video/both	Y ❑ N ❑	
Audio: computer/telephone/both	Y ❑ N ❑	
Pricing model: flat fee/per connection/audience size	Y ❑ N ❑	
Recording output format	Y ❑ N ❑	
Standard pricing	Y ❑ N ❑	
Target audience	Y ❑ N ❑	
Last updated	Y ❑ N ❑	
Maximum attendees	Y ❑ N ❑	

STEP 2

N O T E S

Create a
Project Plan

OVERVIEW

Assign roles and responsibilities

Determine the components of your project plan

Create a template for each type of presentation

Schedule your presentation

Because so many moving parts and variables make up a virtual presentation, it's easy to forget something. Unlike in a live presentation when you can just send someone off to make a copy for you or fetch someone from another cubicle, when you miss something online, it can become a showstopper. At the very least, it'll delay your presentation to the point where your audience loses concentration and you can't achieve your objectives.

A project plan can help. You can't concentrate on what you're doing if you're worried about something else. The project plan is designed to anticipate your needs and those of your audience, help you set up your presentation, and free you to concentrate on your presentation rather than the tasks involved in presenting.

Think back to the first few times you presented live. You probably double- and triple-checked your presentation, practiced diligently, and made sure you got to the room early to scope out the physical layout and the equipment. As you got better, you got more comfortable and probably didn't have to do everything on that mental checklist.

As you get more comfortable presenting virtually, you'll be able to just fire up a web meeting and make it run (practice and rehearsal are still recommended, no matter your experience level). It will happen eventually. For now, let's start by treating each web presentation as a project, breaking it down into its component pieces, and then checking them off one by one so you're relaxed and focused on achieving your goals.

Assign Roles and Responsibilities

Putting on a virtual presentation consists of a number of tasks. A group of people can accomplish these tasks, or they might fall on you alone. Still, the jobs need to be done if your presentation is to succeed. Consider the following full list of responsibilities and tasks, not all of which will apply to your particular situation:

◆ Provide clear goals and objectives to meeting stakeholders; ensure they meet expectations.

◆ Design and build a presentation to fit the tools you are using.

◆ Make sure the chosen technology is functional and you know how to use it.

◆ Invite the audience and inform its members of any necessary preparation.

◆ Rehearse.

◆ Deliver the presentation.

◆ Follow up.

◆ Make sure your audience follows up (after all, that's why you're presenting).

Think about these various tasks and who will perform them. Often, one person (most likely you) will take on many or even all of these roles. Regardless of how many people you have on the team, all of these roles need to be filled. See Step 4 for more about fulfilling these roles and responsibilities.

The Producer

The producer is the "project manager" for the presentation. If you can't quickly identify this person, then it is most likely you. The producer is responsible for making sure the web presentation is planned and delivered and all the tasks are accomplished. This role may be filled in a couple of different ways. Sometimes the producer is also the presenter (and the designer, tech adviser, and coffee fetcher). Other times the producer will simply help wrangle all the disparate pieces of the project together.

Depending on the type of presentation, the producer may fill a different role:

◆ **General webinars and town hall meetings.** The producer does not present but gets everything organized per the project plan. Often the producer introduces the presenter to the audience and sets up the presentation. He or she may simply act as host. Sometimes this role is filled by someone who never speaks on the webinar at all, but is a true "project manager." This only happens in large companies with lots of resources.

◆ **Sales demos and calls.** These often happen on the fly, so although the basic presentation or demo might be put together by a team or someone else, often a producer is not needed.

◆ **Training.** As a trainer, the producer will probably take care of most of the logistics. Serving as host can give you the credibility you need with your audience and let you invite guest speakers or subject matter experts while maintaining your focus as the trainer. Building credibility with your audience is important. Also, you'll probably repeat the presentation more than once, and with practice the logistics will become more automatic and easier for you to handle on your own.

◆ **Marketing webinars.** Even more commonly than with general webinars, the producer of a marketing webinar does not deliver the presentation but ensures its successful delivery to what are mostly large audiences of multiple stakeholders. There is usually sufficient budget to do these.

The Webinar Presenter(s)

As the deliverers of content, webinar presenters need to be prepared, professional, and focused on the desired outcomes. Steps 7 and 8 provide more information on this topic.

Webinar Stakeholders

Account for the stakeholders before you build your presentation to make everyone happy—because you want everyone to be happy. Stakeholders might include the following:

- **Budget holders** (also known as the payer). These may be your organization or a particular department. Offer budget holders the chance for input early, or you could be burning the midnight oil with all of their last-minute suggestions. Getting their buy-in up front helps prevent surprises and misunderstood expectations.
- **Attendees.** It's important to check your assumptions about subject and tone. You might invite a representative from the audience to your rehearsals and involve him or her in the planning.
- **Implementers and salespeople.** These people will interact with attendees following the presentation. Salespeople will get inquiries (if all goes well), and they need to know what to say and how to respond. If you're implementing a new policy, the attendees' managers need to know what's happening, and the people who have to implement the policy want to make sure that the information you give is accurate.

Support Staff

Don't laugh; some people have support staff even if you don't. These people might help you assemble your presentation or send out invitations. Anyone who can help you falls into this category.

Your Audience

These people need to be contacted and told about the event. They might have to do reading or preparatory work (in the case of training), or you might need to gather information from them before the presentation (this is often the case for a sales demo). Follow-up tasks might also be made available. You need to plan for such preparation and follow up before you start presenting.

POINTER

Before planning any web presentation, ask yourself, "Who cares about the outcome of this presentation?" You can save yourself a lot of frustration by asking for potential audience members' help and input before you finalize your plans.

If you identify who cares about each part of your presentation and then plan to make it work for that audience, you'll have a relatively stress-free time and achieve what you set out to do—a good day at work for anyone.

Determine the Components of Your Project Plan

Whether you are conducting an elaborate marketing webinar or a simple web meeting, many components are necessary to consider. How much effort or time you need to invest in them up front depends on the kind of presentation you are delivering.

A project plan reduces the chance of forgetting an important step or detail. It should be filled out and shared with all the stakeholders in advance (this also shows them how much work is involved in this "little project," which can buy you extra resources or at least a little good will). If you are the main stakeholder, it will still serve as a tool to help you cross your t's and dot your i's. Project plans should be kept, as they reduce the need for reworking if you aim to deliver the presentation again.

STEP **3**

Let's look at the general components, followed by templates for each type of presentation:

- objectives and outcomes (Think about yours and those of your stakeholders.)
- audience analysis
- marketing and invitations
- tools and technology
- the presentation itself: whether you build it from scratch or use an existing presentation
- follow-up with your audience to ensure you meet your objectives.

A Word About These Plans

Many presenters feel that they don't need to put a project plan together for every presentation, and they're right. Pilots with hundreds of hours of flight time probably don't need the takeoff checklist either, but they still go through it. Mind you, the consequences of a plane crash are considerably worse than those of a presentation going awry (although it might not feel that way at the time).

As you become more comfortable presenting online, or you do the same presentation or training course over and over, you'll be able to skip, ignore, or modify these plans. By checking these steps, though, you're unlikely to forget something, and going back to the plan from time to time helps make sure you're not missing an important step.

Create a Template for Each Type of Presentation

Planning for a General Web Presentation

General webinars will serve as the base example for comparing the subtle differences among types of presentation. The basic components of any project plan are pre-work, logistics, content, rehearsal (also see Step 8), delivery day, and follow-up.

Pre-Work

Pre-work involves all the thinking and planning you need to get out of the way before you actually build your presentation. Even if you've done this presentation a hundred times, every audience is slightly different, and you can always consider lessons learned to make it better.

◆ Define objectives and outcomes.

◆ Analyze the audience.

◆ Check with stakeholders for their wish list(s).

Logistics

Because most people are least familiar with this part of a web presentation, you will want to take your time when taking care of logistics. It will create the proper relaxed environment for you to conduct a successful webinar.

◆ Assign roles.

◆ Choose platform and tools (if you haven't already done so).

◆ Schedule the event.

◆ Create and send invitations.

POINTER

Some platforms create and send invitations for you while others require you to do a little work. Consider this feature when choosing a platform. Also, save yourself a lot of hassle by choosing a platform that automatically puts the date in participants' calendars through Outlook or Gmail.

Content

Now you're ready to look at the content of your presentation. Whether you're using a presentation you've done before, converting a live presentation to web delivery, or starting from scratch, the thought process remains the same.

◆ Create visuals (not just PowerPoint slides, but documents you might show, screen captures of software, titles for whiteboards, and anything the audience will see throughout the presentation).

◆ Create a script or outline (more on this is covered in Step 7, but if you're used to "winging it," you'll want to use at least an outline the first few times you present online until you get the hang of it).

◆ Create polls and other specialty visuals. If your platform allows you to create polling slides, questions, and other visuals in advance, do so. It will prevent typos and other mistakes that can trip you up.

Rehearsal

◆ Conduct a tech test.
◆ Schedule and conduct a dress rehearsal.

Delivery Day

◆ Secure your environment. (Ensure your physical comfort, defend against distractions, and warn anyone who might think about interrupting.)
◆ Log on at least a half hour early and test (even if you think everything is under control).

Follow-Up

◆ Send out communication as necessary. This includes action items, reminders, and notifications of where participants can find the recording or get copies of your visuals.
◆ Debrief and decompress. While it's still fresh in your mind, capture what went well and what you can do better next time.

Now that you know the basic components of a project plan, you can adjust the plan to fit the specific type of presentation that you are giving. Figure 3.1 is a basic project plan to get you started. Take a look at all the plans here and find the one that will get you closest to your desired outcome—after all, that's why you're doing this presentation.

Planning for Sales Demos

A good sales demo does more than simply ask clients to sit back and watch as you regale them with all the features of a product.

FIGURE 3.1

Project Plan: General Webinar or Meeting

This tool will be a good starting point any time you need to do a basic information-style webinar. Follow the steps to prevent last-minute panic. You'll find more specific presentation plans later in the book.

Because most of us have "real" jobs in addition to making web presentations, why not make your life simpler?

Plan Step	Why It Matters	Time Frame
Pre-work: Define objectives and outcomes Analyze the audience Check with other stakeholders to confirm assumptions	You obviously need to know not only what you want to achieve but also what others in the organization might want to make sure happens. Maybe you should use (or avoid) specific terms, or marketing or legal has wording or format needs. Don't make yourself crazy later.	Especially the first time you do this particular presentation, give yourself plenty of time. I would suggest you begin conversations with stakeholders a month before the event so they know the project has begun and they'd better speak now or forever hold their peace.
Logistics: Define roles and responsibilities Choose platform Schedule event Create and send invitations	If you haven't already chosen a platform for this event, you need time to assess it and get comfortable. You should know its strengths, capability, and drawbacks before building your presentation and finding you've painted yourself into a corner.	If you're just now choosing a platform, you'll need plenty of time. Also, several rounds of invitations might be necessary, so plan to send them out early enough that people's calendars aren't full but not so early they forget about your event. Three weeks is probably about right. Plan accordingly. Also, plan for reminder notices 24 hours and even one hour before the event (someone will have the time zones confused). Ease people's pain and your stress level.

Figure 3.1, continued

Plan Step	Why It Matters	Time Frame
Content: Create the presentation visuals Create a script or an outline Create special visuals	Presenting online is different. You might have to add content like housekeeping rules and how the audience can interact with the platform to chat or write in questions. Additionally, animation that works live might not work on your platform. Your script is your chance to plan for the interaction you would have naturally in a live presentation but can easily forget when presenting online. You want to make sure you don't have any typos in your polling or other visuals that can come from rushing just before the event.	This will depend entirely on whether it's the first time you've given this presentation—or the 40th.
Rehearsal: Conduct tech rehearsal Conduct dress rehearsal	If you are unfamiliar with the platform and its capabilities, schedule some time to play with it and get familiar. Try conducting a poll and using all the annotation tools. When you're comfortable, schedule a dress rehearsal for your actual presentation with the close-to-final content.	Tech rehearsal will depend on your experience level with the presentation and the tools. If you've never given this presentation, a walk-through a week before the event with a couple of stakeholders is suggested to get their input and check your assumptions about content and time. Most important, hold at least one full dress rehearsal at least 48 hours before your event. That way, if you have to make changes, you have a little time and won't freak out the night before.

Figure 3.1, continued

Plan Step	Why It Matters	Time Frame
Delivery day: Secure your environment Log on early	Many presenters become distracted by their surroundings when presenting. Make sure you have time to schedule a private conference room, clear your schedule, or turn off the phones and put the dog out.	Give yourself at least half an hour before showtime to log on and make sure you (and any co-presenters) have everything working and aren't rushed for time.
Follow-up: Send out any communication Debrief and decompress	Remember you're putting yourself through this to accomplish an objective. Don't let action items sit there without a quick reminder to your audience. If you want people to have the visuals, make sure they can get them quickly while they are still thinking about your topic. If you've recorded the webinar, make sure the recording is available and people know how to access it.	The longer you let your audience members go without reminding them of their action items or confirming your seriousness, the less likely they are to take the action you want. Show them you mean business. Any follow-up communication should be conducted within 24 hours of your presentation at the most.

It should be highly interactive and often the shorter, the better. Greatwebmeetings.com conducted interviews of people who sat through sales demos, mostly of software products, which revealed that 60 percent of people who sat through live software demos online were very unsatisfied with the experience. The two main reasons for this unhappiness were the following:

◆ The presentation focused too much on features that the customer didn't care about.

◆ The presenters were boring and long-winded.

Planning can go a long way to avoid both problems.

What's Different?

To be truly effective on a sales call, you can't bore potential stakeholders with what they already know. If you don't know what problem they're trying to solve, you'll find it hard to keep your demonstration on target for moving your sale forward. Because the meeting will be smaller and less formal, you need to build in lots of conversation, have a presentation that's flexible enough to change course on short notice, and be much more casual and improvisational. Because these demos are often set up on short notice, your comfort level must be high.

See Figure 3.2 for how the project plan might differ for a sales demo.

FIGURE 3.2

Project Plan: Sales Demo

With a sales demo, the stakes are high. You don't want to just "wing it." The key things to watch for here are that your platforms allow you to share applications effectively, that you know how to make them work, and that you build in opportunities for interaction and check-ins with the customer. Data dumps are deadly!

Plan Step	Why It Matters	Time Frame
Pre-work: Define objectives and outcomes Analyze the audience Check with other stakeholders to confirm assumptions	Audience analysis is crucial. You don't want to tell people a lot of things they already know or belabor points they don't care about. Knowing what your audience knows and wants before presenting is critical to your sale.	This is tricky, because you should be practiced and comfortable with the tool but be ready to present on a moment's notice. Some platforms allow you to do instant meetings where you can go to a demo while on a sales call with your client. Be prepared.

Figure 3.2, continued

Plan Step	Why It Matters	Time Frame
Logistics: Define roles and responsibilities Choose platform Schedule event Create and send invitations	Most online or virtual sales demos will require access to the software you're talking about. Platforms that allow screen sharing or sharing of your desktop are best for this, but such applications take some getting used to. Learn them before inviting your audience.	Take a week or so to consistently practice sharing the application and using the platform. Then be ready to go on a moment's notice.
Content: Create the presentation visuals Create a script or outline Create special visuals	If your audience found you online, they already know who you are. That's not why they're there. Get to the good stuff as soon as possible. If you can, have examples ready for them so they don't have to watch you log in, rarely a selling feature.	You'll be doing this quickly, and your prospects will tell you they have very little time. They're right. Get to the good stuff quickly.
Rehearsal: Conduct tech rehearsal Conduct dress rehearsal	Knowing your technology is important but not as important as listening to your customer. Be comfortable enough to switch your presentation midstream. Practice as much as you have to.	Give yourself at least five days to practice over and over with your demo, a couple of times a day, until you know it cold and can focus attention on your prospect.
Delivery day: Secure your environment Log on early	Same as usual. Take control of your environment.	No change.
Follow-up: Send out any communication Debrief and decompress	Have you made the next step clear to your audience? Then plan for that step to take place. Don't let leads go cold.	Never let a lead go for more than 24 hours. Immediate follow-up is best.

Planning for Training

Presentations for training and skill development require a higher level of interactivity than general webinars and usually require more on the part of the audience; pre-work and follow-up are often part of the course.

What's Different?

Especially if you're new to web presenting and training, presenting yourself as confident and professional is crucial. Expect more rehearsal time than with any other presentation type. Additionally, you will have to appease some very picky stakeholders.

See Figure 3.3 for how the project plan might differ for training.

FIGURE 3.3

Project Plan: Training

This project plan applies specifically to training presentations. The good news is that training often uses the same content as general webinars but presents it to different audiences, and you can often skip steps (like choosing a platform) after the first presentation.

Still, a few days before a training event, do a quick scan of this plan and see if you've omitted anything. If questions come up that you can't answer, you still have time to prepare yourself. Don't let familiarity make you drop your guard!

Plan Step	Why It Matters	Time Frame
Pre-work: Define objectives and outcomes Analyze the audience Check with other stakeholders to confirm assumptions	In training, you will generally have more stakeholders who want direct input to the process. Also, there is more need to make sure that any changes you make to the visuals and content are reflected in the supporting materials.	Because being an effective facilitator depends on your comfort and ease with participants, your need to master the technology is high. Schedule a ton of practice into your plan.

Figure 3.3, continued

Plan Step	Why It Matters	Time Frame
Logistics: Define roles and responsibilities Choose platform Schedule event Create and send invitations	The scheduling of the event might require coordination with managers and human resources. If there is a learning management system (LMS), the course must be set up there and scheduled on the platform. Invitations must include things like pre-work and prerequisites. The good news is that once you've done this, it's usually just boilerplate for the next time.	This will depend entirely on your familiarity with both the platform and the content. With new projects, give yourself at least four weeks for this process.
Content: Create the presentation visuals Create a script or outline Create special visuals	Remember this is a new environment so you need to create visuals that not only fit the content but also reflect the new environment. Do you need to spend time showing people how to use the tool? Are housekeeping rules different than for the classroom version of the course?	This will depend entirely on whether you're giving this presentation for the first time—or the 40th. If you're the developer, it will take much longer than you think. Trust me.
Rehearsal: Conduct tech rehearsal Conduct dress rehearsal	Your credibility and the reputation of the training depend on your facility and comfort with presenting so you can focus on the learners.	This is up to you and your conscience.
Delivery day: Secure your environment Log on early	Same as usual. Take control of your environment.	No change.
Follow-up: Send out any communication Debrief and decompress	Make sure you plan the little details of what follow-up will be required to ensure transfer of learning and to satisfy the requirements of the stakeholders.	Are specific follow-up activities required for the class? Schedule those immediately so that people know you're serious.

STEP 3

Planning for Team Meetings

If you're planning a team meeting, the goal is to get team members to communicate with each other and with you. They should arrive prepared to get down to business, and you should expect to focus on facilitation, not the tools.

What's Different?

You want people to have as many ways to communicate as possible. Let them chat with you and with each other. Again, command of the platform and functions is vital so that you can focus on moving the group toward the intended goals. Use brainstorming tools like the whiteboard and encourage use of the chat function, which helps spontaneous and innovative ideas develop.

See Figure 3.4 for how the project plan might differ for a meeting.

FIGURE 3.4

Project Plan: Team Meetings

Team meetings use a similar project plan as the others. One important note is to add who is doing what piece of the presentation and how long each piece should take so they don't run long.

Plan Step	Why It Matters	Time Frame
Pre-work: Define objectives and outcomes Analyze the audience Check with other stakeholders to confirm assumptions	The successful outcome of the meeting depends on the agenda and people being prepared. Know what is and is not on the table, and be prepared to hold attendees to it.	Give yourself enough time to get on people's calendars.

Figure 3.4, continued

Plan Step	Why It Matters	Time Frame
Logistics: Define roles and responsibilities Choose platform Schedule event Create and send invitations	What kind of meeting is it: just an update or do you actually have to brainstorm and make decisions? Make sure the attendees know what you expect before they get online.	This depends on how much of the meeting you're going to run yourself and what you're hoping to accomplish.
Content: Create the presentation visuals Create a script or an outline Create special visuals	Don't bore your audience; plan for plenty of interaction. Arranging for open phone lines is the best. Allow others to present as often as possible to keep your team engaged.	Make your presentation long enough to accomplish what you need to accomplish, yet short enough that there is an urgency to get everything accomplished. Anything longer than an hour had better be darned compelling or your team will start to check email and instant messages.
Rehearsal: Conduct tech rehearsal Conduct dress rehearsal	Knowing your technology is important, but you need to focus on facilitating the meeting. Get comfy with your tools, and don't schedule a web meeting when a conference call will do. Use the right tool for the right purpose.	Unless there's something new you've never done, you'd best be comfortable by now.
Delivery day: Secure your environment Log on early	Same as usual. Take control of your environment.	No change.
Follow-up: Send out any communication Debrief and decompress	Action items are critical. Use the whiteboard and other tools like recording and transcribing to ensure everything is captured and communicated.	No change.

STEP **3**

Schedule Your Presentation

A common mistake a lot of presenters make is to lock in a date for the event without thinking through all the details. The reason is not that they don't know how long something should take—it's that they don't have the time in their schedule to do what needs to be done. (If you're like most people, delivering a virtual presentation is not your sole job, but one of many items on your to-do list.)

Start with the end in mind. Know when you want to hold your event or presentation, but don't tell your audience yet. In creating your project plan, you might find that you haven't given yourself time to do everything you need to do. Check your assumptions against your plan and then set the date in stone. A good rule of thumb is to send your invitations three weeks ahead of the presentation (when possible).

Also, do not schedule the rehearsal for the day before the event. If something is not working, you will need more time to make the necessary adjustments.

POINTER
Give yourself 48 hours between rehearsal and the final presentation. This will allow you enough time to make any necessary changes.

Wrap-Up

Because presenting is stressful, presenters need to relax and project confidence to achieve success. As you can see, the level of complexity goes up with a virtual presentation or meeting. By looking at all of the moving parts and having a concrete plan, you can reduce or eliminate a lot of the stress that distracts people and prevents them from being successful.

Remember that even experienced pilots use their checklists before every flight.

◆ Understand the roles and responsibilities associated with presenting and get as much help and input early in the process as you can so you can focus on your presentation.

◆ Now that you know the components of a successful web presentation, you should be able to reduce the time necessary to prepare with each presentation.

◆ Don't expect brilliance the first time, but with repetition and practice comes comfort and success.

Now let's take a closer look at how working with other people can make your job easier.

NOTES

_____

_____

_____

_____

_____

_____

_____

_____

_____

_____

_____

_____

_____

_____

_____

_____

_____

_____

_____

_____

_____

Work
With Others

OVERVIEW

Work with someone else
to ease your load

Solicit feedback from
anywhere you can find it

Work with a co-presenter
to make your
presentation more
audience-friendly

The stress of single-handedly
trying to put on a web presentation (at least until you're
consciously competent at it) can
often lead to giving up. With
many presentations, a lot of
details must be taken care of. If you try to do it all by yourself,
three things will happen:

◆ Other stakeholders will find something to criticize, usually
   at the last minute.

◆ You will not receive objective feedback. Your presentation
   might need just a couple of simple tweaks to be great, but
   without solid input you'll never know.

◆ You won't be happy with the event, no matter how successful it is.

You don't need all that drama. By enlisting the help of others,
you can ensure not only that your outcomes and objectives are met
(happy stakeholders) but also that the presentation itself is less
stressful and more enjoyable, and you'll be at your best.

Work With Someone Else to Ease Your Load

Step 3 outlined the different roles and responsibilities associated with putting on a good web presentation. Now would be a good time to ask yourself, "What are the roles I have to play, and where can I enlist some help?"

Help doesn't necessarily mean formally enlisting people into your project, although that would be nice. It can be as simple as remembering that someone on your team included a great slide in a previous presentation or finding a memorable piece of clip art.

Another advantage of asking people for assistance with your presentation is that you might find more help than you expect. I remember doing a webinar and thinking of it as my burden to bear alone. When I told someone what I was working on, though, an amazing thing happened. Because he was going to have to present webinars himself, he had lots of questions and looked to me for advice. He offered to sit in on rehearsals and look at my PowerPoint deck just to get ideas for his own presentation. This type of peer review is a great resource.

Enlisting help from the right people for the right reasons is also important. Be specific about what type of feedback you are looking for. Otherwise, you may wind up with a lot of last-minute input that can derail your efforts and stress you out unnecessarily.

Think about your stakeholders and ask for their help mainly in their area of influence. For example:

IT department. A lot of organizations make the mistake of assuming that because web presentations involve exchanging information via technology, information technology is the main stakeholder. This is not necessarily the case. Get IT department members' help with technical details such as choosing a platform that will work with your network environment and maintaining network security. These professionals, however, are not likely to be good judges of what presentation features and functions are important to you.

Budget holder(s). Conversely, the people with the budget don't always know what will work best in the online environment. They may insist on unnecessary bells and whistles (the suggestion of video nearly always comes from people who don't have to run the meeting). Don't choose features that add no value. Find out what the stakeholders' objectives are, and then find the best way to meet them while staying true to your goals.

STEP **4**

Check Your Assumptions

Even if you are the lone presenter and the person with sole responsibility for a project, odds are someone else cares about it or you wouldn't have been assigned the task. If you're a trainer, the sponsor of the training (the head of human resources or sales, for example) wants the training to be targeted and effective. The managers of the employees you'll be training definitely want the skills to be transferable to the job, and the end users (your learners) want something meaningful, interesting, and relevant. Checking your assumptions before getting to a final version of your presentation is necessary to make sure you haven't forgotten any critical information or steps. Once you have finalized the content, fixing individual pieces is much more difficult and stressful.

Also, you've put people on notice that this presentation is coming, which, especially with training and marketing webinars, is very important. You want people to eagerly anticipate your presentation. Advance word of mouth will help you bolster attendance.

Finally, the biggest assumption you may make as a presenter involves your web presentation skills. If you're not confident, you may be your harshest critic. A little positive feedback goes a long way to calm nerves and build confidence before you go live. People who are their own biggest fan present a different challenge—they think everything they do and say is brilliant. These folks might need a bit of a reality pie in the face to become aware of their weaknesses. Either way, as my mother used to say, feedback is a gift.

Solicit Feedback From Anywhere You Can Find It

If you think about most web presentations, they have several steps, each of which comes with unique challenges. Getting good input throughout the process will increase the odds of success with each little piece, which will add up to a successful presentation.

Consider the following:

- **Objectives and outcomes.** Once you've identified your objectives and outcomes, check with your stakeholders to make sure your assumptions are correct. If you are a trainer, check with the project sponsor. If you're doing a marketing webinar, check with sales to make sure you are driving the audience to the correct next step in the sales cycle. For example, doing a demo of your product is not sufficient; you need to make sure you include language about how to sign up for a trial account.
- **Invitations.** Think about how you are going to attract people to your presentation. Some people probably have a vested interest in making sure enough of the right people show up to warrant all your efforts. Check with the managers of your intended audience, your marketing department, or even potential employees. Is the objective of the meeting or presentation clear? Are the benefits of attending obvious (do participants understand what they will get by attending)? Are the spelling and grammar correct?

◆ **Visuals.** Visuals are further discussed in Step 6, but at this point you need to think about how to get your message across in a clear and interesting way. Marketing and sales departments probably have better clip art collections than you do, and they may also have previously constructed presentations from which you might be able to lift visuals without having to reinvent the wheel. Ask other people in your department, or review your old sales presentations. Taking existing slides and just copying and pasting them into your new template is easier than starting completely from scratch.

◆ **Your presentation skills.** Presentation skills are covered in Step 7, but for now ask yourself, "Who cares about this content?" and "Whom do I trust to give me honest, constructive feedback?" Then invite some of those people to sit in. If possible, choose people who have presented online, and offer to provide feedback on a presentation in return.

Work With a Co-Presenter to Make Your Presentation More Audience-Friendly

The reasons to work with a co-presenter are numerous. Some of them are obvious, but the greatest benefits might not be apparent. Among the reasons to work with a co-presenter are the following:

◆ Shared workload.

◆ Reduced multitasking. One of you can speak while the other scans chat messages, looks through submitted questions, and tends to any technical errors.

◆ Added credibility. If your goal is to do a series of webcasts as marketing tools or to establish your business's brand, invite guest speakers who will bring in their own audiences and add credibility to your efforts.

◆ As the host, you get to reap the benefits of having people way smarter than you do the speaking.

◆ Stronger audience engagement. Every time a speaker's voice changes, listeners accordingly reengage. Two voices are inherently more interesting to an audience than one person talking for a long period of time.

You can work with a co-presenter in one of two basic ways. The first is to simply have one person act as host, welcoming the participants and handling the housekeeping (such as how to ask questions, chat, or use the other features), and the other person acts as guest, presenting his or her material uninterrupted.

This format is helpful when co-presenters work separately and have limited time to plan and rehearse. The downside is that the presenters are not viewed as equals. The person with the heavier subject matter load will be the "star." Also, forcing the audience to listen to a single voice for a long time is ill advised. If the "main" speaker fails to be compelling, the whole presentation might drag.

The second method is to treat the presentation as an interview. Though this requires more planning, transitioning between two speakers helps the presentation feel more conversational and engaging. Also, the presentation faces less risk of going too quickly. Uninterrupted speakers tend to pick up speed like a snowball rolling downhill. Alternating between speakers allows for pauses and time for your audience to digest your information. These features will be built into the presentation rather than left to the whim and self-control of the presenter(s).

An example of a co-presentation is presented below. Having completed the introductions and housekeeping, the speakers are ready to move into the main content of their presentation:

Speaker 1 (bringing up the visual for the next topic): Nancy, can you share with us the problem with the Romanian silkworm?

Speaker 2: Sure, I'd be happy to. The biggest problem right now is that . . . [the speaker continues for no more than two or three visuals], and that's the challenge for all of us.

THE ULTIMATE IN CPLP™ TEST PREPARATION

ASTD LEARNING SYSTEM

Your self-paced, self-directed CPLP™ study guide with 10 complete volumes detailing the entire body of knowledge for the workplace learning and performance profession.

CHECK YOUR KNOWLEDGE! THE ASTD LEARNING SYSTEM COMPANION STUDY TOOL

Track your test prep progress with 650+ interactive questions to check knowledge, review content, uncover opportunities for improvement, and understand rationale behind answers.

ASTD LEARNING SYSTEM FLASHCARDS

For faster learning and longer retention—250 color-coded cards filled with 500 questions, definitions, and graphics to customize your study experience.

Order all three of the above CPLP™ test preparation resources in one comprehensive package and save.

10 volumes / CD-ROM / 250 Flashcards

Product Code: 180812

Member Price: $504 (reg $563.95)

List Price: $674 (reg $753.95)

Visit www.store.astd.org and search by product code 180812 to order.

100819.6220-9535

Speaker 1: Well, I can see why we should be concerned, but I'm sure the question a lot of us are asking ourselves is, "What can we do about it?"

Notice a few key things about this approach:

◆ It's designed to be conversational. Audiences listen and relate better to conversation than to formal speech.

◆ The questions are designed to be asked as often as every two to three slides or visuals. This allows you to get on a bit of a roll and bring a topic full-circle before getting interrupted, but doesn't allow you to just take off without pausing and letting the audience digest what you've said.

◆ If done poorly, it can sound somewhat fake or like a bad news anchor team ("And that's why the congressman re-signed. Over to you, Bill."). Rehearsal is needed so that you don't feel the need to read everything word for word.

POINTER When working with another person, planning for transitions and handoffs is important. This will avoid uncomfortable silence and prevent you from speaking over your co-presenter, and vice versa. To do this, make sure each person knows the points the other will be making. Writing a full script (more on this in Step 7) isn't necessary; instead, write out the last thing you're going to say as close to word for word as possible. When you say your last line, the other person will know to pick up his or her part.

Wrap-Up

Remember the story of the "Little Red Hen"? No one wanted to help her make the bread, but everyone wanted to help her eat it. It's the same with getting help for your web presentation. For most of us it will be a chore in addition to whatever it is we do with the rest of our workday. It might be hard to find people who can help, but it's worth the effort.

STEP 4

First, be willing to take all the help you can get and don't be afraid to ask. Second, plenty of other people in your organization have a stake in a successful outcome, and you aren't doing them or you any favors by waiting until after you've delivered the presentation to determine if you've hit the mark or not.

Work with others to lighten your load and improve the finished product. Here are some suggestions:

◆ Take an offer of assistance. Work as a team and allow people to feel they have a vital part in the presentation and and a stake in its successful outcome.

◆ Identify the right people to help, and promise your assistance to them when the time comes.

◆ Make requests for help; you're likely to get a better outcome than you'd get by doing all the work yourself.

◆ Try co-presenting the first time or two until you're comfortable. Your audience will appreciate it.

NOTES

Create Compelling Content

OVERVIEW

Compel people to attend your presentation

Build a presentation that engages and maintains interest

Get tips for using examples and "war stories"

Encourage participants to take action

Every great presentation deserves an audience, and every great audience deserves a presentation that delivers on its promises. This section looks at creating a compelling story so people will want to attend and organizing content in a way that engages people and moves them to take the desired action, whether learning a skill, implementing a new policy, or buying software.

A great presentation, on the web or otherwise,

◆ is about something people want to know or have become interested in

◆ looks good

◆ is delivered professionally

◆ inspires people to take action.

If your presentation lacks any of these elements, something is wrong. If your content isn't relevant to your audience, you won't be able to deliver a great presentation. If your presentation has interesting visuals and the package is slick but at the end of your time with audience members they just shrug and say, "Not for us," then as far as you're concerned, you gave a good presentation but not a great one.

In other words, great presentations are compelling. Compelling is often defined as "forceful, demanding attention, or convincing"—about as good a description of an excellent presentation, training seminar, or meeting as could ever be found.

As a presenter, you want to compel your audience in two ways. First, you want participants to show up interested in what you have to say and eager to learn more. Then you want them to take the desired action or learn the desired skill.

To compel them to show up, you must design the presentation with the audience members in mind. A well-thought-out invitation tells them what to expect and how to attend. Finally, you must deliver on your promise with a presentation that engages them throughout and drives them to take the desired action.

Compel People to Attend Your Presentation

You're a great trainer with a fabulous message. Your product is revolutionary. But why should audience members take time out of their hectic schedules to listen to what you have to say? No matter how experienced you are or how great your message is, people will not attend your presentation unless you give them a compelling, concrete reason to do so.

Let me tell you about someone who just didn't understand this.

When I first started www.greatwebmeetings.com, a prospect complained that he couldn't get anyone to show up for his free marketing webinars. He had paid a developer for world-class visuals (I could only dream of creating such great slides!), his presenters were slick, and he had a product that, if people tried it, had a great closing ratio. But he could not get enough people to sit through his marketing events.

I knew the problem as soon as I received the first invitation to an event. The email invitation read, "Learn all about the exciting new features of _____ Software, Version 2.0." It then listed a number of the product's new bells and whistles and why it was so fabulous.

The problem was that all of the benefits involved the presenter and had nothing to do with the customer. People had no reason to drop everything and register, just to learn about a new software program. (I don't know about you, but I have enough software on my computer already to last a lifetime.) The name of the software wasn't compelling or interesting—I didn't care, and neither did most of the folks on this client's prospect list. If they did care about the product, then they were already customers and didn't need to sit through a "get to know you" web event.

Make the benefit of attending the presentation clear in your invitations. Make attendees' jobs easier. Save them money. Save them money while making their jobs easier. Just give them a good reason why they should care about what you're telling them! Before you construct an invitation or put your presentation together, write, in a single sentence, what people will get from attending your presentation.

◆ "Learn four ways to clear your ears after swimming" is so much more compelling than "Why Earcleaner Formula 4 is for you."

◆ "Hear our CEO outline what your job will look like for the next year" is more interesting than "Visit our town hall to hear the CEO speak."

You've done a lot of thinking and analysis. Time to put it to use. Compel people to attend by telling them what to expect and what great value they'll get in exchange for their time. Don't just get them to show up—make them want to show up. It all starts with the invitation.

Whether formal or informal, a good invitation should contain the same basic ingredients:

◆ the content of the presentation
◆ the type of audience it is designed for

- how it will benefit members of the audience
- when it will occur
- how to connect to the webinar or web meeting. (Make this as painless as possible please.)

Answer all of these questions, and your audience will show up predisposed to listen to what you have to say, if not to take your requested action.

Presentation Length

Maybe the most controversial question my clients ask me involves presentation length, because no firm answer is available, and it largely depends on the presentation you're giving. Here's what I know: People can't pay attention online for as long as they can in a live setting. Some of this results from common human courtesy—people tend to be respectful of presenters and others speaking in the same room. When they don't have to look a speaker in the eye, however, clicking "leave meeting now" can be a great temptation.

In a future step, you're going to build your presentation. Now is the time to seriously think about how long it will be. Take this into consideration before you even open PowerPoint. Once you get started it's almost impossible to stop adding content. Remember you want it to be informational enough to be compelling, but not so padded or over-done that people leave before it's finished. Consider the wisdom in the old adage, "leave them wanting more."

When was the last time someone complained a webinar or webmeeting was too short?

Your presentation should be as long as necessary but not one second longer. To determine exactly that length, follow these guidelines:

- **The more distractions your presentation includes, the less participants will pay attention.** People are easily distracted by their surroundings. If you deliver your presentation in a quiet place where people are free to focus on it, you'll have more mindshare than if too many other things are available to look at. People may also be distracted by their stomachs (avoid presenting just before lunchtime) or traffic concerns (at the end of their day, people might get impatient). Understand what might distract your audience and either address those concerns or plan for them in your presentation.

◆ **A good length for most presentations is 45 minutes.** Depending on the goal of your presentation, most members of the audience will do their best to accommodate you for about 45 minutes. Here's where that number came from. Mentally, people block time in hours. If your meeting fills a one-hour block, they can prepare to focus for that long (if you're interesting and engaging). Assume you'll start a minute or two late and finish a minute or two before the top of the hour so people don't stress about their next appointment. That leaves you about 45–50 minutes of pre-sentation time, including a question-and-answer period.

◆ **Sales presentations and demos make up the exception to the 45-minute rule.** Ironically, sales demos are best kept short. The number-one complaint of people who sit through sales demos is their excessive length. If you're a salesperson, you know that in the best meetings the client says, "You have 10 minutes, so make it good" and you're still there 40 minutes later because the client is engaged and asking questions. Answer such questions as quickly as possible, make your point, and move on. Tell your clients that you just want 10–15 minutes of their time, and if the presentation goes long because they want to know more, then good. Focus on the "sales" part of the phrase, not the "demo."

◆ **Think of your learners.** Deciding on the right length for a training session is very difficult. A common mistake is to simply move a whole presentation that was built for in-class delivery to the web. No one I know (presenter or audience) can comfortably withstand four or eight hours of online training. You're better off breaking those modules into smaller blocks and scattering them over a period of time. The American Red Cross Disaster Services, for example, divided a 14-hour instructor-led class usually delivered over two full days into five 90-minute chunks scattered over two weeks. As a rule, my training sessions tend to last 90 minutes—longer than the 45 minutes I specified earlier but not so long that people can't focus if they're really interested and engaged. As the presenter, I take responsibility for making that time well spent. In general, a couple of shorter, more focused sessions are preferable to a single long one.

STEP 5

POINTER

Plan to have enough visuals to fill your entire presentation time. While the trend in live presentations (thankfully) is to reduce the number of PowerPoint slides, web presentations are different because if you don't change the visual regularly, people tune out, less engaged than they would be in a seminar hall, conference room, or class. Online, the visuals should change frequently. Do not let more than three minutes go by without the audience seeing something new, even just a highlighter or an arrow pointing to the bullet point under discussion. If you show the same visual for more than five minutes, you're probably letting good points go without visual reinforcement, not to mention losing your audience. Make sure you visually reinforce all key points so the audience will remember and retain them. Please note this is not permission to bludgeon people to unconsciousness with PowerPoint slides; just be cognizant of what the audience members will be looking at and how you will keep them interested.

Simple and Effective Webinar Invitations

Studies by web platform providers including BrightTALK indicate that the more steps it takes to respond to a webinar invitation, the less likely people are to take advantage of the opportunity.

The need to set the audience's expectations to get results is actually rooted in science. According to Dr. Ellen Weber of the blog at www.brainleadersandlearners.com, uncertainty or stress about attending a meeting causes the amygdala to fire with multiple stress signals, increasing defensiveness and reducing audience members' attention span. Let them know what's coming and that it won't hurt a bit.

Email is the best way to let people know about a webinar. Whether they receive a fancy formal invite or an email with a link that says "click here," people don't want to work too hard. Remember the following tips about effective emails:

◆ **Links are critical.** Telling someone to go to a web address and register won't work. Marketers will tell you that for every click people have to make after the first one, you'll cut your potential audience in half.

◆ **If you're asking people to register in advance, do it all on one webpage.** Enrolling in something that's supposed to be convenient shouldn't be a hassle. Don't ask for every piece of information in advance.

◆ **Add a calendar function.** One of the biggest problems even otherwise intelligent people face is adding or subtracting hours to accommodate different time zones. If your invitation simply says "11:00 a.m. Eastern," you can bet someone in San Jose will show up at 2:00 p.m. Most platforms now have a function in their setup that creates a link for people to put the date directly into their Outlook or Gmail calendars.

Figure 5.1 is a sample invitation for a basic marketing webinar, the kind you get from potential vendors all the time.

You can tweak this invitation format to work for the following kinds of presentation:

◆ **Sales demos.** Very informal, sales demos are usually done at the request of the customer. The trick here is to state

FIGURE 5.1

Sample Email Invitation—Marketing Webinar

This invitation assumes that your audience is more interested in the topic than the presenter. Unless you are a well-known industry leader, you might want to take this approach—after all, most people you send this to will have no idea who you are yet! Notice the email is to the point.

Subject Line:
3 Ways to Empty Your Email Inbox—A New Webinar

The Body of the Email (start with a catchy statement that will show up in the preview pane of recipients' email, so those who scan their email will at least know they should pay attention to this message):

Studies show that email is now the biggest time waster in the workplace. How can you make better use of your time, reduce rework, and get more done?

Join us on _____ at _____ for a webinar: "3 Simple Techniques to Clear Up Your Email Inbox." [The presenters from your company] and the authors of *What Part of "Delete All" Did You Not Understand?* will give you practical advice on how to manage your email, communicate more effectively with your teammates, and save your manager's sanity.

Register now by clicking here. [Link directly to your landing/data capture page.]

In this webinar you'll learn [insert your learning objectives here]:

♦ why email has gone from timesaving tool to the bane of your existence

♦ 3 simple techniques to stop email from sucking up so much of your time

♦ resources and tools to help you keep up the good work.

[Include a two-sentence bio for each presenter.]

[Include a one- or two-sentence overview of your company and its achievements.]

Don't forget to join us for this important event [provide date and time].

Register here [repeat link to landing/data capture page].

[Personalize your signature and include your title (president, CEO, chief marketing officer)].

Contact Information and Website Info:
We respect your privacy. To take your name off our email list, please click here [include an email link] and put REMOVE in the subject line.

This invitation contains everything you need. You have a problem that needs to be solved (email clutter) and an identified audience (those who need help). You have identified what will happen and who will help them, and you have made it as easy as possible to register their intention to attend.

No matter how well you craft your invitation, if your webinar is a free marketing event, you will have about a 50 percent no-show rate. Putting links to automatically enter the calendar information into attendees' email helps, but it won't solve the problem. This presents another good reason to record your webinar and make it available after the fact—people were interested enough to sign up, so others will probably take advantage of the opportunity.

the benefit to the customer, so instead of "Let's do a demonstration so I can show you all the features," try "You can see what it can do for you and how it will help solve your business problem."

♦ **Training**. One big challenge is getting people to sign up for training. Try some unique twists. First, make sure the benefits speak to your audience members personally ("You'll learn . . .") and to their organization (". . . so that your team will . . ."). Second, try bribery. If attendance at the webinar goes on participants' record as "professional development," make sure they know about it. CEUs (continuing education units) and PDUs (professional development units) make great enticements to attend training events. If you've ever worked with project managers who belong to associations like the Project Management Institute, you will know that PDUs are like pirate doubloons to those folks—they'll do anything to attain them, even sit through webinars.

♦ **Team meetings**. The key to successfully inviting people to team meetings is a good agenda. An agenda gives people all the information they need to come prepared to be productive, active participants in the meeting. As an added bonus, having an agenda allows you to eliminate claims of ignorance when people show up unprepared.

Figure 5.2 provides an example of a simple but effective agenda that you can include with a meeting invitation.

FIGURE 5.2

Meeting Agenda Template

Save this information as an email template, and just fill it in for each new meeting. Don't miss this step—you'll be surprised how much smoother your meetings run when people know what to expect and act accordingly.

Time, date, and meeting length

Meeting format and log-in data

Include both web and audio requirements and if people will be expected to participate by voice.

Meeting host and presenters

Objectives and outcomes

Describe the meeting—for example, whether you will be updating participants on a critical piece of information, asking them to brainstorm (in this case advise people what to think about in advance), or asking them to make a decision.

Expected participant preparation

Note whether participants need to read, prepare, check out, or analyze anything to be properly armed for the meeting.

Where participants can find relevant information and materials

Ensure that all participants have a copy of the spreadsheet you sent. If not, they can find it on the shared drive or the SharePoint site drive (include a link so they don't have to bug you for it).

Any additional information they should know

Introduce any new people or outsiders who will be participating in the meeting. Note anything new or different about this meeting relative to the others you've held.

Build a Presentation That Engages and Maintains Interest

A presentation that doesn't accomplish its goals can still be good, but not great. Crafting strong, dynamic content is necessary for a presentation to hit its mark. Some important elements of a compelling presentation include the following:

◆ creating an introduction that puts the audience at ease

◆ getting to the point as quickly as possible

◆ making your presentation relevant

- using the right tools
- keeping it short
- knowing what you're going to say and when
- leaving the audience with a succinct wrap-up and a clear action item or next steps.

If this seems a bit overwhelming, see Worksheet 5.1 for a planning tool that takes all this information into account and lets you simply fill in the blanks.

Welcome and Introduction

Getting your presentation off to a great start is critical to your success. Your audience might be apprehensive about what's to come, and when people's brains are stressed and their amygdalae are firing warning signals, it's very difficult for them to relax and appreciate what you're telling them. As a presenter, you'll also want to ease your fears about them not responding.

What are *they* so tense about? After all, you're the one presenting. These are some audience concerns:

They are unfamiliar with the platform. Ease any participant anxiety by giving a quick tour of the platform and its features. In particular, introduce any interactive features you plan to use early so that participants actually become engaged with the technology.

- Explain the chat rules you have set. Will participants be able to chat with each other privately, just publicly, or only with you?
- Describe how you will take questions. Will you provide a separate box for typing questions, or will you simply be using the chat feature? Will the phone lines be open? What about participants raising their hand to get your attention? Depending on the platform and the kind of presentation you choose, you might need to carefully show audience members how to do this so they're confident about their ability and won't be intimidated.

◆ Share the annotation tools and whiteboard. Does your platform let you share the annotation tools (circling, highlighting, putting an X on the screen)?

If you expect attendees to participate, make sure they know how and are comfortable. Don't assume that they know what to do. More important, many people have only been on the receiving end of one-way web meetings and don't expect to participate. Make your presentation the positive exception.

They think this will be a waste of time. Most people have had bad experiences with boring or inept webinars. So have members of your audience. If they come in with a bad attitude, they'll not be positively disposed to you and your message. Your greeting should put them at ease. Make sure you provide an agenda and a timeline. You'll want them to have the agenda before the presentation or meeting (it might entice them to show up!), but you'll also want to have an agenda slide in your presentation. You're going to promise to make good use of people's time and deliver on that promise.

Your purpose is unclear. Very early on in your presentation, you should put any concerns or distracting questions about audience members' roles to rest.

They don't know what to expect. I find that a single slide with some directions (which I just copy from presentation to presentation to make it easy on myself) is sufficient. You'll want to list the following:

◆ **Suggestions for eliminating distractions.** This includes having participants turn off email and instant messaging. Both audience and presenter should turn off other software running on their computers. For you as the presenter, it minimizes distractions and ups the odds of people paying attention to you rather than their email. For the audience members, though, every application running on their computer reduces bandwidth and can result in their computer running slowly (which creates annoying lag time in the presentation) or even freezing and crashing.

◆ **How you'll take questions.** Will you take questions throughout the presentation (I would hope so, at least a couple) or hold them till the end? Will you open the phone lines or have participants submit their questions in writing?

◆ **Presentation length.** Help participants set expectations to prevent them from stressing about making their next phone call or attending their next meeting.

They don't know who you are. Your introduction should establish your credibility and make a good human connection. Let participants know why they should bother listening to you. Give a relevant piece of experience ("Like you, I have been in sales for more than 10 years, especially in the health sector with accounts like GE Medical") and then stop bragging. They want to know you're qualified, but not your entire résumé. If you have a webcam, let them put a face to your name. At the very least, you'll want to provide a good candid photograph of yourself so they are aware of the actual human being on the other end. Try to avoid posed, professional head shots unless you're giving a high-stakes, big-money webinar or sales demo. If your photo looks stiff or too formal, you may put your audience in the wrong frame of mind. You want people relaxed and participating, not intimidated.

A General Introduction

Here's a sample of an introduction with very specific language. Try it on for size, and then keep honing it until it sounds like you. The important part is not the exact words you use but how professional you sound and that you don't leave out any critical information. You want to know what you're going to say so you can set a high standard right from the first word.

(Your webcam appears. It gets turned off before the presentation so the audience doesn't see you scratching, drinking water, or panicking when something doesn't look right.)

INTRODUCTION: Good morning, everyone. My name is
_____, and I welcome you to our webinar training session on _____. We'll be together for the next _____ minutes or so, and that will include lots of time for your questions. (If participants don't know who you are, give a short overview of why you're qualified to present this topic.)

HOUSEKEEPING (including a slide with this information in bullet form): Let's take care of some of the administration. First, please turn off your email and instant messaging. Not only will this help you concentrate, but it will free up bandwidth on your computer to help prevent crashes. We will be taking questions by phone, and you can also use the chat feature to write your questions down as they occur to you.

TOUR: For those of you who have never used this web meeting platform before, in the lower right-hand corner you'll see the chat box. In fact, you'll see that it says "Chat with all." If you'll just click your mouse into the box on the bottom and type where you're from, everyone will be able to see it, and we'll know everything is working. Please do that now. We'll also be using some of the other tools, and I'll explain how to use those in just a moment. If you want to expand the screen to full screen, you can click the "full screen" view icon—it looks like a TV screen with an arrow on it in the upper right-hand corner. I'll give you a moment to do that . . . great. To restore it, just click that button again.

AGENDA (it's always a good idea to have the objectives written on a visual and an agenda slide with the goals bulleted): Our goal today is to [show objective slide] show you the benefits of _____ and how to take advantage of that to make your job easier. Specifically, we'll cover _____ [show agenda slide], and it will take about 45 minutes, including time for questions and answers.

STEP **5**

Polling is a great way to kick off a presentation or meeting to let you know what the audience knows and wants to know. It is also a fun way to get them interacting with the technology as quickly as possible. Ideas for great kick-off polls include

- What brought you here today?
- How much experience do you have with _____?
- Have you ever attended a training or meeting by webinar before?

TRANSITION TO FIRST ASSESSMENT OR TOPIC: Now, let's find out a little bit about you. I'd like to show you the polling feature, and I'm going to ask you . . .

FOR SALES PRESENTATIONS (The biggest mistake salespeople and demonstrators make is showing the client too much information. The following simple introduction will help you understand what the customers need from you so you don't bore or overload them.): Thanks for joining me today. In our time together, I plan to show you _____ and _____ because you said you were interested in that. Before I just start poking around, why don't you tell me what you're specifically looking to learn or if you have things you're particularly interested in? That way we can make sure you're getting the most from our time together.

Now that you've made a concise, informative introduction, you're ready to move on to the body of your presentation.

The Body of Your Presentation

When putting together the core of your presentation, you want to include critical, persuasive information but don't want to turn your presentation into a data dump or simply overload your audience with detail. Before you even fire up PowerPoint, ask yourself the following questions, and then create the visuals and other content that will support your objective.

◆ **What should I know about my audience?** This includes what audience members know about your topic and what

Especially for new presenters, webcams can be a distraction. Try using them at the beginning to say hello, help people recognize who you are, and establish a rapport with your audience, and then turning them off when you get into the "meat" of your presentation. That way, if you check your notes, scratch your nose, or need to take a sip of water, you won't feel self-conscious.

their attitude is toward it. See the Audience Analysis Checklist in Step 1 (Worksheet 1.1) for the kinds of questions you should ask yourself. If you don't know the answers, try to find someone who does—such as your predecessor, someone who's presented to the group before, that person's manager, or your peers.

◆ **What do I want my audience to know about this topic?** If someone were to tell you that you could only pick three or four key points to support your objective and persuade your audience, I'll bet you would know what they are and why they matter to your audience. Make that the cornerstone of your evidence, argument, or pitch. More evidence is not always better; sometimes it just overwhelms your audience. Stick to three or four main points and save the rare examples or oddball objections for the question-and-answer period.

◆ **How will I visually display the information?** Decide what pictures, charts, or graphs you'll use to support your case. People will remember your key points best if you support them with congruent visual images and your spoken or written words. If you use a graphic, make it easily understood and clear. Unclear or seemingly unrelated images just confuse the audience. If you find it helps to "storyboard" your presentation, print out your visuals and lay them out on the floor or table to see if they flow together and connect to tell a coherent story.

◆ **How will I transition to the next topic?** Many presenters run out of steam when they've completed a visual and aren't sure how to move smoothly to the next topic. This results in awkward pauses and run-on sentences that sound less than professional. One way to avoid this is to plan precisely what you're going to say that will wrap up the topic you've just discussed and bring the audience along to your next point.

A quick note about transitions: You don't want to say the same thing each time you switch visuals. Most people have been to a presentation where the speaker says, "Moving on" or "On this next slide you'll see" until they can almost say it along with the speaker. Mildly annoying, it also reduces the speaker's credibility. Write out each transition so that you'll know what you want to say and avoid repeating yourself. Mix and match the following five basic types of transition statement, and then write cues to yourself on what to say for each transition:

◆ **Ask questions.** Take this opportunity to get members of the audience to raise questions or points of discussion to make sure they're tracking with you. Ask, "Does everyone see how this ties to our goal of reducing waste?" and then, while you pause for a response, move to the next visual.

◆ **Answer questions.** If people have submitted questions by chat or writing, take this as a great chance to pause, let them digest what you've told them, and see if a relevant question appears in the queue. This also allows you to make sure they understand the last point before you take them further along and maybe confuse them totally.

◆ **Make short statements or offer amusing trivia.** One way to transition and keep the tone light is to finish your thought and then offer a short statement or piece of relevant trivia. For example: "You know, many people find that they save 30 minutes daily by answering email only four times a day instead of throughout the workday." Then let the next visual come up and continue.

STEP **5**

- **Just be silent.** If you're talking all the time, members of your audience won't be able to digest what you've told them and may get overwhelmed. Sometimes when you make a key point, it's best to just let it sit, advance the slides, and start clean on the next thought.
- **Check in with your audience.** If you're running a meeting, some participants probably haven't contributed yet. Take some time to check in with these folks ("Robert, we haven't heard from you on this; what are you thinking?"). If you do this regularly and naturally, it not only promotes participation and allows the quieter audience members to contribute but keeps the entire audience on its toes and from answering email. No one wants to be caught daydreaming or not paying attention.

Be sure to write the types of transition statement down, though. When you start presenting, it's easy to focus on the content or the technology and forget about your transitions. By writing them down and putting them in your script (more about this in Step 7), you won't be likely to forget them when the pressure's on.

Worksheet 5.1 is a simple, general template that will help you plan your presentation. The nice thing about this is once you have filled it out, you'll know exactly what visuals to provide and how much information is necessary without overstuffing your presentation. Your audience will appreciate it.

Get Tips for Using Examples and "War Stories"

When creating content, think about the examples you will use and the stories you will tell. Remember to tailor this to your audience. The people who have to learn a new software system have a very different set of things they need to know and care about than the people who are paying for that software.

Keep the following things in mind:

◆ Use participants' language, not yours. If they call employees "associates" in their company, then, by golly, call them associates.

◆ Use recent stories. People don't care what happened years ago; they care about the present. Unless you are a historian, you should by now have stopped using case studies that start with, "During the Reagan administration."

◆ Keep success stories and examples relevant to participants' world. If they come from a small company, explaining how IBM uses your product might be counterintuitive (after all, they can't pay what IBM pays). Conversely, a large customer might not find what you can do for an individual relevant.

◆ Explain acronyms and any jargon. If you don't take the time to explain that ROI stands for "return on investment," you can bet someone will take the time out of your presentation to ask you what it means. Don't let anything distract your audience from your message.

POINTER

If you find yourself saying, "Oh, by the way" a lot during your presentation, it means you're probably adding too much detail and overwhelming the audience. Plan what you're going to say and save the extra examples for the rare but cool instances that may come up during the question-and-answer session.

Encourage Participants to Take Action

You've laid out your evidence, you've established your credibility, and your product or topic is amazing. Don't let the audience off the hook. You want people to take action—whether to try a new skill, put your product on their shelf, or get out there and sell version 2.9 of your product.

Make sure that you have at least one visual that outlines the next step. Write it out, clearly and plainly. There should be no question in audience members' minds what you expect them to do. If multiple steps are required, be sure to provide them in bullet form, which is short and precise. If you want participants to return that evaluation by Thursday the 13th, make sure they know you want it back by Thursday the 13th.

A good idea is to have that visual available before you go to a question-and-answer period, and again after. You'll tell participants what's expected of them, which should raise questions; you'll answer those questions; and then you'll remind participants of their action steps or what will happen next.

Wrap-Up

Remember, you want to motivate your audience to attend your presentation, focus on the topic of discussion, and prepare the audience to engage with you and then take the desired action. You want to compel people to attend and (even more important) to take the desired action or next step after they've seen and heard your presentation.

Because members of an audience aren't bound by the same rules of common courtesy during an online presentation that they are during a face-to-face meeting or speech, it's up to you to give them the motivation to show up, pay attention, and be enthused.

By carefully planning your presentation before you actually build it, you'll identify what's critical to include. Even more important, you'll discover what may be information overload, irrelevant, or distracting. You'll also be able to plan to overcome audience objections in advance.

WORKSHEET 5.1
Presentation Outline Template

Presentation Topic _____

Estimated Time _____

Start Time _____

Presenter(s) _____

Introduction:

♦ Introduce yourself and your background or credentials (via picture or webcam, for example).

♦ State the topic of the webcast and desired outcomes or action items.

♦ Tell attendees how long the webcast will last.

♦ State any special requests, prerequisites, or prework they'll need to complete in advance of the presentation.

♦ Lay out the ground rules.

♦ Give the participants a "tour" of the platform and introduce the technology you will use.

_____

_____

_____

_____

_____

_____

Topic or agenda item 1: _____

Visuals or media required: _____

_____

_____

Questions or interaction you'll use: _____

_____

_____

Estimated time: _____ Time marker:_____

Worksheet 5.1, continued

Topic or agenda item 2: _____

Visuals or media required: _____

_____

_____

Questions or interaction you'll use: _____

_____

_____

Estimated time: _____   Time marker: _____

Closing statement: _____

_____

_____

_____

_____

Call for action items (write this out completely so you get it right and your audience understands): _____

_____

_____

_____

Create Visuals That Support Your Presentation

People are primarily visual creatures—they take in most information through their eyes. This is both the good news and the bad news of presenting online: Information that's interesting to look at and relevant to your presentation will stick with your audience. Information that's distracting or hard to look at (or even annoying) will get in the way of your message.

The beauty of an online presentation is that it provides a richer experience than just a phone call: You can show pictures, demonstrate processes to your audience, and answer participants' questions in real time, all while helping them retain the information and moving you both closer to your objectives.

Poor visuals that make you appear less than proficient with your media do not help at all. Put simply, good visuals

- ◆ tell the same story to the audience as your words
- ◆ reinforce your message and move the audience toward your objective
- ◆ look professional and add to your overall appearance of credibility
- ◆ are easy to work with.

STEP 6

Prepare a first visual for when participants log in to the meeting. A professional-looking, colorful slide makes a good welcome. (Your platform probably offers a couple of ways to do this, but the simplest is to have the first slide of your presentation loaded and ready to go.) Use this slide to make your first impression. Simple text on a white background won't convey to audience members the interesting experience they're in for.

For the purposes of this book, the term visuals describes anything the audience sees while your presentation is going on. This includes the things you don't want people to see.

When we talk about visuals in this book, we'll discuss five primary things people see during a webinar:

◆ webcams
◆ pictures and screen shots
◆ PowerPoint slides
◆ annotation tools
◆ shared applications and documents.

To be used to its optimum, each item has both unique qualities that can add value to your presentation and challenges that need to be overcome.

Use Webcams

The quality of webcams and streaming video is quickly changing. Some platforms support these features well (iLinc, Netbriefings, Telenect), others use them well in their top-tier packages (Live Meeting and WebEx), and some don't support them at all yet, but that will probably change (GoToMeeting and GoToWebinar). This will become part of your presenting arsenal, but check your computer, your web platform, and your audience's resources before making it a permanent part of your presenting repertoire.

Just the act of asking participants to focus will often buy you a few minutes of precious time to grab their attention. People mean well, and if you explicitly ask them to pay attention, they will often comply—for a minute or two. After that, it's up to you to grab them and keep their attention where you want it, or their email or what's going on out the window may become more interesting.

Webcams are a feature that presenters both love and fear. People who are good, experienced live presenters believe that webcams will make the presentation closer to a live event because people can see them. They are pretty cool—after all, anyone who grew up with *The Jetsons* couldn't wait for the day when video phones would be in every home and office and audiences could see presenters in all their glory. (Those of us who've been to video conferences at six in the morning quickly learn this is an overrated feature.)

Webcams have various downsides:

◆ They suck up a lot of bandwidth and cause screens to freeze and applications to crash (though this is improving).

◆ They capture everything—even things you don't want the audience to see.

◆ A feature of most inexpensive webcams, including those built into today's laptops, is a fish-eye lens, which means you really need to stay in the one place it focuses effectively and keep motion to a minimum. If you've ever looked through the peephole in an apartment door, you know what this looks like. Even when the face is in focus, the hands look like they belong on a sci-fi movie monster.

◆ Members of your audience often concentrate on the visual of you on a webcam (after all, it's shiny, and things move) rather than your content. Unless your ego is completely out of control, you don't want that.

STEP **6**

◆ Webcams are just one more thing to worry about. When presenting online, your goal is to reduce the number of distractions, not have to stay on top of more things. You want to be able to focus on your audience and your presentation.

When does a webcam add real value to a presentation?

◆ Video reduces the feeling of distance between participants and presenter and builds a connection.

◆ It can increase audience comfort. People's brains make decisions about buy-in and acceptance very quickly. If they see you and the impression is positive, they lower their defenses and are able to pay more attention.

◆ Good webcam visuals send the signal to your audience that you are technologically competent and comfortable. This technology is still new enough that many people are impressed by the wow factor of seeing the speaker on their computers. If this is important to your image, then you should find a platform that supports webcams.

Webcams become more trouble than they're worth when they

◆ cause technical problems by sucking up bandwidth or over-taxing your computer

◆ distract the audience's attention

◆ divert your attention away from the task at hand.

Follow these eight guidelines for using webcams effectively:

◆ **Make sure participants can see you.** If you plan to use a video camera, the attendees should be able to see who's talking. Just like taking pictures with a still camera, the light source should be in front of you (natural light through a window or at least from a lamp) so that your face is lit. If light is coming in from behind you, your face will be in shadow and your audience will have difficulty seeing you clearly.

◆ **Don't move around too much.** Most plug-in cameras aren't designed for high resolution. Mix that with how hard your computer is already working, and you'll find that sudden movements will cause the picture to blur or even break up. This usually solves itself when you get to the new position, but it causes a couple of seconds of useless video.

◆ **Be aware of what you wear.** Leave aside your personal fashion sense for a moment. Clothes can cause havoc with your webcam. Pure white clothing can "flare" and show up very brightly on camera, which can wash out your face. Also, checked patterns don't read well on camera and can look blurry. Wear a solid-color shirt but preferably not bright white.

◆ **Dress appropriately.** People form opinions of a speaker based on what they see. Depending on the location of your audience, you might be presenting during nontraditional work hours or from home. Remember, though: It's still a presentation. Dress appropriately for the audience. Here's a hint—most webcams only show you from mid-chest up. You'd be surprised how many people wear a jacket, a dress shirt, and cargo shorts!

◆ **Watch out behind you.** Always test your camera positioning before going live. Look behind you—you don't want your audience watching people walk past your cube. Nor do you want that fern in the corner to look like it's growing out of your head. Ensure that your surroundings look professional to your audience. In my home office, where I do most of my webinars, I have an old-fashioned bookshelf that's crowded with books. I am told it looks very impressive and professional. Fortunately, no one's asked if I've read all those books.

◆ **Look your audience in the eye.** Just as in a live presentation, eye contact is a sign of trustworthiness, competence, and confidence. The problem is that your audience isn't in the room. As a result, remembering where to look is often a challenge. Many presenters wind up looking at either their own picture on the screen or, if they're using two-way video, the faces of their audience. The problem is that on camera it appears that you're looking down or to the side, which is not your intention.

Most webcams have a little dot of light that tells you where the camera is—treat that as your audience's eyes and speak in its direction.

◆ **Be prepared for calamity.** Occasionally, the webcam will just freeze up and stop working. No one will be able to tell you why, and tech support providers will shrug and say they don't know either. That's OK. Just be prepared. Most platforms allow you to post a still picture of yourself that will serve as a placeholder for where your webcam video would be. Make sure you're smiling—candid shots are perfectly fine as long as you look happy and you're not doing anything incriminating.

◆ **Use this tool sparingly.** My clients find this may be the most useful tip of all: Use the webcam to greet your audience, introduce yourself, and establish rapport. Then, when you get into the meat of the presentation, turn it off. Save bandwidth, don't worry about what you look like while presenting, and let the audience focus on the content of your presentation. You can earn extra "brownie points" if you turn it back on for the question-and-answer session with audience members so they can see your confidence and professionalism. You can also look them in the eye as you sign off and leave them with a positive impression.

Find and Use Pictures to Tell Your Story

Human beings like pictures. More than that, people need them to help solidify ideas. They can understand the concept of a flower, but to really understand one, and to tell a rose from a tulip, people need to have that visual information in their mental repository.

The good news about web presentations (in fact their best feature) is the ease with which you can show people what you're talking about using more than just words. If you want to convince people how easy logging in to the human resources system is, you can actually show them the system and step by step how to log in to it. If your presentation shows the difference between a correctly filled-out order form and whatever it is people have been turning in—voilà: your message in all its glory.

Here's what you need to be aware of:

◆ **Remove the picture once it has fulfilled its use.** A picture will get the audience's attention, but if left on the screen, it can become a distraction. Don't put a picture on your audience's screen until you're ready to talk about it. Then remove it before it steals attention.

◆ **Keep the images relevant.** Be careful about putting a picture up just because it's pretty. People try to make sense of new visual information, and putting up a picture just because you think you need one may confuse them or provide a conflicting message (such as a smiling person when you're talking about IT problems).

◆ **Use photographs and screen captures over cartoons.** Most clip art packages contain lots of colorful artwork ranging from pictures of ringing phones to wacky cartoon-style pictures of people. In general, people find these less credible and professional than photographs.

◆ **Make sure the people in your pictures look like your audience.** To really improve your credibility and your professionalism, make sure the photographs you use are relevant to your audience. This includes obvious items like a diverse range of ethnicity, genders, and ages. Recently, a client of mine was doing a webinar for prospects in China and replaced all of the pictures of people in the company's standard presentation with pictures of Chinese, or at least Asian, people.

◆ **Use candid photographs over professionally staged pictures.** Nobody believes that those perfectly groomed young people in the cool clothes represent you or your employees (sorry). If you can't find the right clip art or stock photos, don't be afraid to take digital photographs of people actually using your product or your employees in action. As long as they're well lit and in focus, people will enjoy them.

STEP 6

◆ Stay legal. If you're making money off the product, you have to pay for the pictures. Photographs are easily available, but the people who took them deserve to get paid. If you're charging any money for your presentation or using it for commercial purposes, please either pay for the pictures or give credit through a Creative Commons license.

Finding Pictures and Photographs

The easiest way to get pictures in a hurry is to use the online clip art gallery that comes as part of Microsoft's PowerPoint (see Figure 6.1). (You can use other tools as well, which we'll talk about in a moment.) If you're in PowerPoint or online, simply click on "Insert," "Picture," and then "Clip Art," and set the category to "Photographs."

FIGURE 6.1

Online Clip Art Section

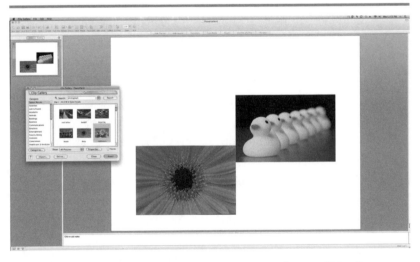

If you have the budget or don't mind paying a couple of dollars for a great picture, you can find other photographs at sites like www.everystockphoto.com and www.istockphoto.com. The gold standard of photos, including celebrities and current events, is Getty Images or Corbis Images.

If you're willing to give credit—which means a small line of text under the picture listing who took the photo and that you're using it through Creative Commons license—you can find a ton of cool photos from folks who use Flickr images through the Compfight website. (See Figure 6.2 for how that looks.) Simply go to www.compfight.com; set the search to "Creative Commons," "On," and "Commercial;" and pick away.

FIGURE 6.2

Flickr Creative Commons License

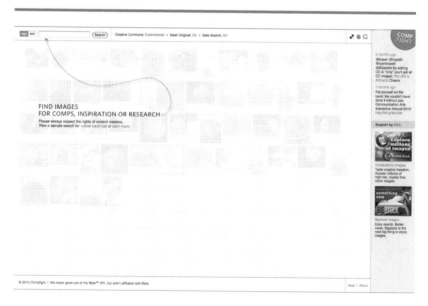

Source: Image courtesy of Compfight. Copyright © 2010. Image from http://www.compfight.com /search

POINTER

Unless you're going for artistic effect, make it easy on members of your audience by having a relevant title or caption for your pictures so participants can immediately connect what they're looking at with what you're telling them. In PowerPoint 2007 you might want to use the "Title and Content" or "Picture with Caption" features under the "Insert New Slide" and "Format Slide Layout" tabs.

Use PowerPoint Effectively

Let's get this out of the way early. You can use other presentation programs besides Microsoft's PowerPoint. A couple you might be familiar with are Apple's Keynote and OpenOffice Impress. These tools are all very similar, so while this book focuses on PowerPoint because about 90 percent of businesses use it, you can apply the information in this section to other presentation programs.

You will learn how to use the tool to build presentations that engage your audience and move you closer to your objectives. Step 7 looks further at presenting effectively with PowerPoint.

Presentation programs allow you to create and use three critical tools:

◆ text slides
◆ charts and graphs
◆ pictures and screen shots.

Text Slides

Text slides are the most useful—and the most widely abused—feature of these tools. They allow you to put words on a page and share them with your audience. This is good, because you want to focus your audience's attention and give people a visual cue and reminder of your topic. However, slides can be overwhelming and open the door to too much information that your audience can't possibly absorb and become "death by PowerPoint."

STEP 6

Consider the following points to make the most of these tools. Remember, these are guidelines, not hard-and-fast rules:

- **Use more slides than you would in a live presentation.** Because your audience is looking for visual stimulus, the changing of slides actually reengages your online audience, and the additional information helps reinforce your message. For example, in a live presentation you might have three bullets on a single slide that remains posted for more than five minutes. Online, you want something to happen onscreen much more often, so you might show a slide with three bullets, followed by one slide per topic with more information. It will still take five minutes to cover the material, but your audience will not be looking at a static slide the whole time. Do not take this as permission to overwhelm your audience, though. Visually support your key points, and don't give people extraneous information; they physically and mentally can't handle it.

- **Tell a story with each visual.** Don't cram too much information on a single page—it's more than your audience can absorb. You should be able to look at each slide and say to yourself what it's about. The next topic will be another visual.

- **Use bullet points instead of blocks of text.** When your audience members look at the screen and see a lot of text, they will automatically stop listening and focus on the words. Give them enough information to let them know what's coming but not so much that they lose concentration; this helps "keep them with you" and focused on where you want their attention. Many presenters use a simple rule of thumb: four bullets per page, four words per bullet. If you need more bullets, that may be fine, or it may be a sign you're covering too much information on one visual.

- **Title each slide and then complete the sentence.** One way to make sure you're simplifying your slides effectively is to create a title for each slide as if it were the beginning of a sentence; then each bulleted piece of information completes it. For example, see Figure 6.3.

FIGURE 6.3

Text Slide With Title and Bullets With Explanation

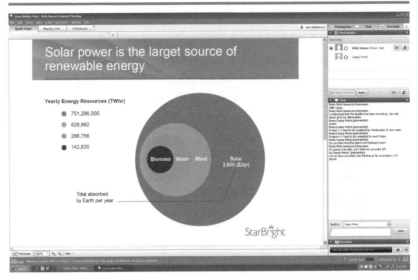

STEP 6

◆ **Check your animations carefully.** Many presenters like to use the animation features so that bulleted items appear one at a time. If you do that, remember two things: First, many platforms lose that capability when you upload your slides. Always check your presentation before going live to ensure you don't get unpleasant surprises. Second, try this simple work-around: If you have three bulleted points you want to make, create three slides—one with the first bullet, another with the first bullet in regular font and the second bullet in bold, and yet another with the first two points in regular font and the third point in bold. In reality, you will be showing three different slides, but to your audience it will appear as if the bullets magically appear on command.

◆ **Don't use crowded backgrounds and templates.** Often the presentations you make online are given to you by marketing, training, or another department, and they involve all kinds of standards. While we don't want you to get fired over this, remember that your goal is to present the information visually to your audience with a minimum of distraction. If every slide contains a logo plus a series of photographs and visuals along the bottom, for example, it can be a bit busier than is useful. Keep distractions to a minimum.

◆ **Don't get too creative with fonts, styles, and colors.** Most important is that the audience quickly processes and stores the information you're sharing. You can spend a lot of time mucking around changing the defaults in your graphics package without adding any value. Most graphics packages use simple rules for creating templates: Light writing on dark backgrounds, dark writing on light backgrounds. Audiences can most easily read such sans serif fonts as Arial and Calibri, usually the default settings anyway.

◆ **Avoid altering font size.** The default fonts in most PowerPoint templates are defaults for a simple reason— they work. For title and text slides, size the title in 44-point font and the body of the text in 28 or 32. If you find yourself adjusting the font size, you may be trying to cram too much information onto a single visual.

◆ **Avoid bulleted lists for special features.** Sometimes you might want a block of text. For example, when quoting someone, it makes sense to show the whole quote (with the attribution). If it's important to show the company's mission statement, include the whole thing. Center the block of text in the middle of your screen and set your font so that you can read it comfortably, starting with the default settings and then enlarging or shrinking it, depending on how much information you have to show. One other tip is to display the quote in large text and who said it in smaller text underneath, but that's a matter of style.

STEP **6**

Guidelines for Charts and Graphs

Whether delivering a sales presentation, trying to get a project passed, or explaining a decline in revenue over the past quarter, one of the strongest uses for virtual presentations is the mix of your insight and the cold, hard facts. Graphic evidence that supports your objective is very impressive to your audience. You want to help the audience members understand your data and move them to the desired action.

For that reason, the way you display evidence must be simple, on-target, and easy for your audience to digest. Even more than with text, your viewers might wander down their own trail if you don't keep them focused on the task and information at hand.

Four Elements to a Good Piece of Visual Evidence

No matter what type of graph you use or what type of information you want to deliver, your visual should have four elements to make it easily understood:

- **A simple, clear title.** Show the audience what you are talking about.
- **Clearly labeled axes or headings.** If you're showing sales results over time, one axis will be money (represented in currency) and the other axis will be time (in quarters, in months, or however you break it down). Your audience should be able to take one look at your graphic and understand your point.
- **A clear legend or explanation of variables.** If you're comparing three sales teams, they should be distinguishable from each other, and viewers should be able to separate one piece of data from the other at a glance. For example, if you're comparing sales results by quarter, identify each team by color and clearly indicate that on the screen (East in blue, West in red, and so on).
- **One story per slide.** Don't try to cram too much information into one visual. First of all, entirely digital presentations use no paper. Second, you'll overwhelm members of

STEP **6**

your audience and risk losing or alienating them and undermining your effectiveness.

In addition to those four elements, you may employ animation and builds to help walk your audience through your logic. One cool feature of virtual meetings and webinar platforms is that you can introduce the information piece by piece to guide your audience toward the desired conclusion. For example, try introducing an empty graph, with just the axes; then introduce the first quarter's results, those of the second, and so on. This will keep the audience engaged and on point. (Remember, if animations don't work in your platform, you can create multiple slides to produce the same effect.)

Create Interaction With Annotation Tools

When you give a traditional presentation, you might use a chart and colored markers, write on the board, or use color to highlight key information (see Figure 6.4). You can do the same thing in almost all virtual presentation platforms. These are called "annotation tools," and they include features that both you and your audience can use to draw attention to key information or offer input. They include:

◆ "highlighting" tools in different colors
◆ "shape" tools that allow you to easily circle or place boxes around key information. Some also include "stamps" like check marks, stars, or Xs

FIGURE 6.3

Close-Up View of Dimdim Annotation Tools

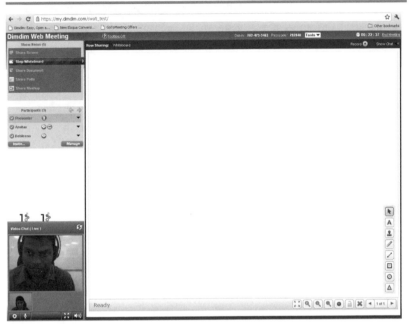

Source: Photo courtesy of Dimdim.

◆ "text" tools that you can use to write on slides or your whiteboard—and allow your audience to do the same if you choose.

These tools are great for creating interaction with the audience and adding life to static visuals. Imagine being a member of the audience and having to look at an unchanged PowerPoint slide or screenshot for more than three minutes. Would your mind start to wander? Can you understand why things like email or texting become a tempting distraction? Many presenters avoid using simple interactive features because it increases the amount of work and requires multitasking skills. However, these tools are a core competence for any online presenter, and they need to be learned and integrated into your presentation. In Step 7 we'll take a closer look at how to use these tools effectively.

Share Applications and Documents

One of the most powerful—and frequently underutilized—advantages of virtual presentations is the ability to share, in real time, anything you as a presenter want to show your audience. This means you no longer need to send PowerPoints in advance and wait for everyone to get on the right page or find where they filed them in their email. You can work with your team to create a budget and input information directly into the spreadsheet with everyone watching and contributing. If you want to show how a new software application works, you can take them right to it. You can even hand control over to a member of the audience to test how well he or she has learned the skill you're trying to teach the group.

The trick, of course, is to understand what you can do as a presenter, and then reach a comfort level with the tools that lets you present and think at the same time (which, surprisingly, is not as easy as it sounds). You'll learn more about the possibilities—and pitfalls to avoid—in Step 7.

STEP **6**

Wrap-Up

The real effectiveness of a web presentation stems from how well you combine the audio and the visual to create a rich experience for your audience. With a little careful planning, you can choose the right tools for the job, present them effectively in a way that supports instead of detracts from your credibility, and move your audience toward the desired outcomes.

◆ Use webcams to build relationships.
◆ Find and use pictures to tell your story.
◆ Use PowerPoint effectively.
◆ Enlist the power of annotation tools.
◆ Share applications and documents.

Now that your presentation is taking shape, let's look at how to sharpen you presentation skills.

Sharpen Your Presentation Skills

Make what the audience sees appear smooth and professional

Ensure that what the audience hears is engaging and effective

Interact with the audience

At this point, you should feel nearly prepared to deliver your presentation. After all, you have

◆ planned the material to be as concise and effective as possible

◆ designed the visuals to work with the tools at your disposal

◆ targeted your audience

◆ determined where all the interaction should go and built it into your delivery plan to reduce the chances of forgetting something.

Audience members gauge the power of a presentation based on two factors:

◆ **What they see.** This includes onscreen annotation tools, PowerPoint visuals, and shared applications.

◆ **What they hear.** This includes your vocal qualities like tone, pitch, speed, and volume.

Think in terms of a great traditional presentation. No matter how compelling the content, audience members will find it really hard to concentrate and listen if the presenter is constantly saying *um* or is standing in front of the projector so the presentation appears half on the wall and half on his or her shirt.

STEP **7**

For experienced presenters, learning to present online is a matter of degree. Presenting live and presenting virtually are similar—the latter just uses slightly different muscles. Compare it to the difference between playing tennis and badminton. Both are racquet sports with similar goals, but they're not exactly the same.

For inexperienced, or even uncomfortable, presenters, you're in luck—you have fewer bad habits to unlearn, and you don't even have to leave your chair. You can sit in a comfortable spot and drink a glass of water, and no one can see you wearing your lucky socks.

Make What the Audience Sees Appear Smooth and Professional

People are visual creatures, so a great deal of the value they derive from your presentation and their initial reactions to it will be based on what they see. Good-looking visuals are a great start. How you work with them, how you integrate them into the flow of your presentation, and your ease with the platform also matter a great deal. Remember that what the audience sees isn't what you see. As the presenter, it's your job to help participants navigate around and get the most from the tools. As you can see in Figures 7.1 and 7.2, the audience isn't looking at as much of the control panel (or dashboard) as you are.

Learn to look smooth and in control while
◆ transitioning between PowerPoint slides
◆ using annotation tools such as highlighting, text, and stamps
◆ sharing applications and programs.

A Note About Participant Controls

Besides what the audience will see, you might also want to control what the audience can do with the tools. You don't want people getting restless and suddenly using their drawing tool to put a moustache on your picture. (On second thought, you might. When doing training, I encourage that kind of silliness to get participants comfortable with the tools and encourage constructive interaction. Let your conscience and the content guide you.)

Most platforms have a "participants' controls" tab, where you can set what you let them do with each tool. For example, you might want them to be able to chat with you to ask questions but not with each other. With large marketing webinars, sometimes with hundreds of participants, you want people to be able to send you questions and comments that you or your designated assistants can read, but not send disruptive messages out where everyone can see them.

When it comes to audience permissions, most new web presenters want to control everything. On the one hand, it limits the amount of multitasking you will have to do and keeps you focused. On the other hand, it makes for a passive presentation

FIGURE 7.1
Participant's Control Tab

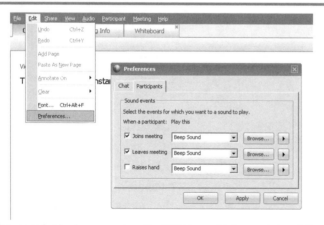

FIGURE 7.2

Presenter Versus Participant View

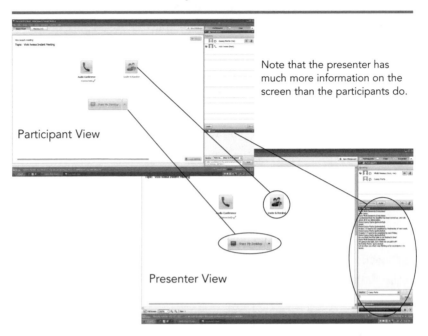

Note that the presenter has much more information on the screen than the participants do.

Participant View

Presenter View

STEP 7

POINTER

Remember, when giving instructions to your participants, some of them may not be familiar with your platform. Others will know it better than you do and want to show off, but don't let that throw you.

and reduces its overall richness and effectiveness. Your audience members can't take part if you don't let them.

Moving from one visual to the next should be fairly straightforward. After all, you push the arrow, and the slide magically appears on your audience's screens. In the real world, though, this simple operation can create a couple challenges for presenters.

First, you can only hope that what you see is what your audience sees. Second, transitioning from one slide to the next (which usually means switching topics) presents an opportunity for dead air and a loss of concentration.

To make sure that the audience sees what you see, set up a second computer. Use the first to log in as yourself (the presenter); use the second to log in as a participant. This provides a huge advantage because with most platforms differences exist between what the presenter sees and what the audience sees.

This gives you the edge in two ways:

◆ Clearly describing for participants how to perform functions like raising their hand and chatting is easier when you can see what the audience sees.

◆ You can see how quickly what you do on your screen shows up on theirs. Lag time often occurs between when things change on your screen and they change for your audience. This is especially true for annotation tools and when you make changes to documents and the whiteboard.

Loading Your Slides

Web presentation platforms fall into two camps: those that ask you to "upload" your presentation to their servers and those that broadcast directly from your computer screen. WebEx, Dimdim, and Live Meeting, for example, ask you to share your PowerPoint slides. GoToMeeting, Glance, and some others ask you to have your presentation open on your computer and share it when ready. Frankly, which platform you go with doesn't really matter—just know that with the "upload" version, you'll usually have less chance of your computer slowing down, but you'll also lose some of the functionality (especially animations and video).

For Uploading-Type Platforms

All the common platforms have a "share presentation" (or "share presentation or document") button on their toolbar. Simply click that button to get a Windows browser. Locate your file on your computer and double-click. It will automatically open in "slide show" view.

For Sharing Platforms

Such platforms as GoToWebinar have a button on the control panel that says "share content." Open your PowerPoint presentation and minimize it so you can see it on the task bar at the bottom of your computer screen. Click the drop-down menu to find the name of your presentation. Some platforms will give you the option of showing the presentation without showing your task bar. Whenever possible, take that option—nobody needs to know the content of your computer.

Transitioning Between PowerPoint Slides

Moving from slide to slide is actually pretty easy. Most platforms have an arrow icon that points either forward (to move the slides forward) or backward (to go back). Some platforms have an upward- or downward-pointing arrow that does the exact same thing. Put your mouse on the button and click once. Voilà: You should see the next PowerPoint slide.

Skipping Ahead and Between Slides

Often you will want to move ahead quickly from one slide to another, skipping visuals you've built and planned to use. Maybe you are running out of time and need to do some editing on the fly, or someone asks a specific question and you want to find the right visual.

If you can, avoid simply clicking quickly through the slides until you find the right one. First, this looks unprofessional and creates awkward pauses. The bigger problem is that you can actually cause technical problems for your audience. When you present a visual, all that information goes from the platform provider through the Internet to your audience's computers. Whether you're showing a visual for 10 minutes (let's hope not) or a split second, skipping ahead quickly can cause lag time, delays, and even crashes that can ruin your presentation. As you can see in Figure 7.3, the thumbnails let the presenter see the

STEP 7

next few slides in the series to transition smoothly from one to the next. You can easily skip ahead by double clicking on the slide you wish to go to, without scrolling through all of them and irritating your audience in the process.

Find the slide you want to show and click it once. It will appear on the audience's screens, without revealing that you're jettisoning your regular presentation. Depending on your platform, you can do this in one of two ways.

The first is most common. A drop-down box shows you the name and slide number of whichever visual is on display. If you click the drop-down box, you can simply scroll up or down until you find the slide you're looking for and click it.

The other way involves using the option to show the "thumbnail" version of the slides along the side or bottom of your screen. When using platforms such as Dimdim, I use this option a lot,

FIGURE 7.3

Dimdim With Thumbnails

Note that thumbnails appear along the side.

Source: Photo courtesy of Dimdlm.

because it allows me to actually see the next few slides. This helps cue me as to what's coming next and enables me to make smoother verbal transitions from one visual or topic to the next.

Transitioning Verbally

Step 5 discussed writing out the transitions you're going to use. By planning your transitions in advance, you can avoid some of the most common challenges presenters face. These include

◆ going blank and forgetting what slide is next. This can result in dead air or worse, the audience hearing you muttering to yourself.

◆ using the same words every time. Phrases like "Now let's move on to the next topic" are fine. If you use them for every transition, however, it will drive your audience slowly mad.

◆ finding out it takes a second or two for the audience to see the new visual, and filling it with clever comments like *um*.

The rhythm to presenting new visuals goes like this:
1. Finish the visual you're on.
2. Click to the next visual as you make your transition statement.
3. Pause; take a breath. Intermittently, check with your audience. "You should be seeing a slide with a picture of a horse—everyone see that?" Participants can chat with you, raise a hand, or just tell you verbally. Once you have the timing down, you should be fine, although one or two check-ins, especially during a long presentation, are a good idea.

Annotation Tools

One of my favorite features of web presentations are the "annotation tools." These features add color and life to static presentations, help your audience engage in and retain critical information, and boost your credibility as a presenter.

No matter how focused and well intentioned your audience is, or how important the topic, staying riveted to a single visual for a long time is a lot to ask. The average person will start looking around after 30 seconds and be completely bored within a minute or two. (With senior executives, you have about half that time.)

While changing visuals frequently helps keep the audience engaged and support your points (don't expect participants to remember everything you talk about without some visual reinforcement), in reality sometimes you will speak to a single visual or series of bullet points for more than a couple of minutes. Give people something to look at after a minute or two. Almost every platform has annotation tools that allow you to add a splash of color or visual interest, even if the visual itself doesn't change.

These tools can include
◆ highlighter, drawing tools, and arrows
◆ stamps, such as check marks and Xs
◆ text tools.

Annotation tools can make the difference between a static snoozefest and a useful, engaging presentation. Notice in Figure 7.4 that in this case you have a choice of pointers, text, different stamps and arrows and can even choose your color. No matter which platform you use, it's important to take the time to understand exactly what you as a presenter can do with it.

FIGURE 7.4
Annotation Tool Bar

Highlighter, Drawing Tools, and Arrows

You will use these annotation tools more often than any others. Follow these tips for using them effectively:

♦ **Spontaneously highlight words and information.** Sure, you can use PowerPoint to underline text and use bold fonts to tell your audience what's important. But, something more compelling comes from a sudden flash of green underlining the information as you say, "Here's what I want you to remember": the appearance of spontaneity (even though you've carefully planned its use). You can also use this tool, among other functions, to trace your route on a map.

♦ **Settle on a color for your annotations before the session starts.** Most platforms assign a color for your annotation tools when you log in (usually the same color as the little dot beside your name on the participant roster). The problem is that the default color might not work with your presentation. If your PowerPoint has a dark blue background, the yellow highlight pen won't show up well at all. During rehearsal, choose the color that looks best, and as soon as you log in to the presentation, select the color for your tools.

♦ **Give the impression of animation.** In live presentations, presenters often take advantage of PowerPoint's animation features to build a bulleted list—hiding the next bullet until they've completed their discussion of the current one. This often doesn't work online, but no problem. Use your annotation tools to check off the bullet you're talking about, and then move on to the next one and do the same. This way, if you spend a fair amount of time on a particular slide, a jolt of color and action will catch the audience's eye and help reengage viewers who might start to slip away.

♦ **Use the precision tools for precise work.** Even with a real felt-tip marker, I'm a graphic idiot. Trying to circle something smoothly using a mouse and a cursor is a lost cause. One of my favorite annotation tools is the circle feature. With a little practice, you can quickly drop a perfectly neat, round circle around text or important parts of your visual without using squiggly, distracting lines. You can nail this with a little practice. It looks slick and takes less work than trying to use the highlighter or pencil tool.

◆ **Arrows beat little red dots.** Sometimes you want to point to specific information on a spreadsheet or at a particular area of your visual. In a live presentation, you might be tempted to use a laser pointer. Some presentation platforms actually have a laser pointer feature that uses a little red dot as a cursor, but using an arrow may be more effective. Take care not to continually move the arrow, as that distracts the audience. Point at what you want, and then take your hand off the mouse.

◆ **Don't talk and draw at the same time.** The single biggest cause of losing your place, besides those horrifying *ums* and *uhs*, is trying to do two things at once. Using annotation tools effectively makes you look professional and slick. Using them clumsily or throwing yourself off by doing two things at once can definitely work against you. Get into the following rhythm when using your tools:

1. **Finish what you're saying.** "And that's why we need to shear the llamas. Now let me show you something . . ."
2. **Pause.**
3. **Select your annotation tool in silence, and move your cursor where you want it.**
4. **Make your mark.**
5. **Resume speaking.** "As you can see, some people shear little designs in the critters."

Talking while using these tools will often trip you up for another reason. Your voice will tend to follow your eyes. As you look in one direction for the right button and then turn in another direction, your audience will hear your struggles.

Stamps

Most platforms have tools that allow you to make Xs, check marks, and other indicators on your screen. You can use these tools not only to enhance your presentation but also to involve your audience. Here's how:

◆ **Check off your points one by one.** Add emphasis to your points by checking them off as you go. Simply choose a stamp or symbol, such as a check mark, and as you finish each point, check it off. This adds color and motion to bulleted slides you spend a lot of time on.

◆ **Let the audience vote.** During training, a great way to turn a simple discussion into an assessment exercise is to let audience members vote by using their own stamps and annotation tools. Depending on your platform, you have a series of choices ("Which of the following is the right action to take under these circumstances?" for example) and let the audience members use their X stamps to vote. This engages people physically and allows you to assess their buy-in or understanding. Make sure you practice this before trying it with a live audience. When it works, it works great. When it doesn't, it can frustrate the audience and create more stress than you need.

Text Tools

The text tool provides a great way to inform members of your audience of some facts and then ask them a question. You can use the text tool (usually represented by a large T) to type in the answer, making it appear on the screen as if by magic.

The text tools are usually best used in conjunction with the whiteboard feature. If you're using a really robust platform like WebEx's Training Center, you can even break up into small discussion groups or "break outs." Then you can use the whiteboard to write down your answers or brainstorm suggestions.

◆ **Add a splash of spontaneity.** Give the audience members information, and then ask them a question by typing directly onto the whiteboard or slide. Have them type out their answer to test understanding or buy-in.

◆ **Color helps identify who said what.** Most platforms assign a color automatically to each participant who is going to use text or annotation tools. This allows you to know who made what suggestion or wrote which answer. If people really object to being identified with pink letters, most platforms let them choose their color but that can be time consuming.

◆ **The text tools can be a bit chaotic if everyone writes at once**, and many presenters maintain tight control over who is allowed to use it. Be sure to practice with this tool as it tends to take a while for text to show up on other people's screens. This can be frustrating at first.

Plan for which tools to use when—and practice. The simplest way to look good using the tools is to plan for their use and practice using them in every situation. Spontaneity may be grand, but most presenters will either stumble around (possibly losing credibility) or, much more likely, get caught up in presenting and forget to use the tools at all, lowering the overall impact of their presentation.

Sharing Applications, Webpages, and Documents

One of the great, and often underused, features of web meetings is the ability to share—not just pictures of software you're demonstrating or documents you're working on but the real thing. Something about this engages the audience.

The ability to see how something works in real time helps a viewer understand the product on a deeper level than just looking at static pictures. A team leader can enhance buy-in by inputting people's contributions into the document as discussion goes on. Here emerges the true potential of the presentation platform as a unique tool in itself, and not just a poor replacement for being in the same room at the same time. Yet, many presenters shy away from using this to its full advantage.

Share the actual document or application at the following points in your presentation:

♦ **You see the actual functionality of the application will increase understanding and buy-in.** Saying that your software is intuitive is one thing, but actually demonstrating and letting the audience participate in its use is something else entirely.

♦ **You really want or need audience input.** In a live presentation, the discussion becomes much more compelling when you use a flip chart or otherwise capture participant input. Now imagine working on a budget in Excel. If someone thinks he or she should spend more money on travel, you can input the suggested number and see the impact on the final budget right away. You can generate some great energy and cooperation by using this feature well.

♦ **You're training people on processes or procedures.** Telling your audience how to log in to a website and start using it is easy. Actually calling up the website and letting participants fill in the information themselves is something else. People learn by doing, not by listening and taking notes. Facilitating audience participation can boost the effectiveness of your training exponentially.

Sometimes you shouldn't attempt to share applications or documents, for example in the following situations:

♦ **You are leery of the bandwidth your audience is working with.** Of all the tools in your new presentation kit, application sharing (especially showing video) hogs the most bandwidth. If you suspect your audience may have poor connectivity, test this in advance and have a back-up plan in place to use if needed.

♦ **You are unfamiliar with the technology yourself and unsure what it will do.** Showing off your expertise with software is one thing; demonstrating that you're not so sure about it yourself and damaging your credibility is quite another. A major exception to this rule occurs when the whole idea is to poke around with a tool as a team, perhaps to evaluate it or get people's input.

STEP **7**

You should know a couple of things before sharing applications and live documents with your audience:

◆ **Test it first.** Members of your audience need to have a pretty fast Internet connection (at least DSL) and all their pop-up blockers off. Test and test again with people on a different network or behind a different firewall than you are. If you have remote teammates, test your web platform with them before conducting a high-stakes presentation of any kind. Once you know it works on their computer, this tool can be very effective and engaging.

◆ **Be aware of the lag time** (the time between clicking a button or moving something on your end and the audience's screens reflecting that change). Move slowly and methodically. The faster you go, the more likely screen freeze or frustration will occur.

◆ **Check in with your audience members on a regular basis to make sure they see what you want them to see.**

◆ **Don't show the audience members more than they want to know.** For example, when demonstrating a piece of software, you need not take them through the log-in process (odds are they know how to do that); take them instead to the first relevant piece of information as quickly as possible. Logging in prior to the start of your presentation helps you prepare.

◆ **Having the audience provide you with information that then appears onscreen is powerful.** For example, showing them a completed form or spreadsheet is one thing, but asking them for the information and then showing it onscreen serves much more like a live demo or brainstorm—and the information better relates to them because it's their information.

Tips for Sharing Applications or Documents

Start at the first important step. Everything you show the audience slows the bandwidth a bit. Don't tempt fate or test people's patience. Everyone has logged in to a software program at some point. Start at the first visual that will actually keep audience members' attention.

Move slowly and deliberately, especially when going through websites (or anything with links). Remember that every visual you show goes to your audience's computers no matter how long you stay on it. If you are searching a website, for instance, and have to click through a couple of links to get to the screen you're seeking, know that your audience will still have to load each page to get to the visual you want.

Don't talk and drive at the same time. Surely you see the pattern by now:
1. Tell them what you're about to do.
2. Pause.
3. Click.
4. Resume your demonstration.

Use your annotation tools to point out important features. If you want people to pay attention to particular features of the application, highlight them using your annotation tools. Point out important links and where participants can find the help screen. Use the highlighter or circle tool to indicate specifications or features that are important to the success of your presentation.

POINTER

A gap of a couple of seconds will always occur between telling your computer to share an application or your desktop and audience members receiving it. Always tell the audience what is happening and what to expect; for example, "Now I'm going to share my desktop. You'll see your screen go all green for a moment, and then you should see www.greatwebmeetings .com appear. Do you see it now? Just chat 'yes' if you see that website on your screen."

By practicing, taking your time, and not multitasking more than necessary, you can take full advantage of these presentation tools and look professional doing it. Remember this type of presentation is not about technical wizardry but about moving people toward your objective!

Ensure That What the Audience Hears Is Engaging and Effective

Any presentation, online or not, comprises three elements: visual, verbal, and vocal. Depending on how rich and robust your visuals are, a greater proportion of the impact must be carried by what the audience hears. Your verbals and vocals are what you say and how you say it.

Verbal content is defined as the word choices you make and how you interpret your content for your audience. Vocal content is the tone of your voice, the speed at which you speak, and the ease with which the audience can actually hear you.

Verbal Content

What audience members hear has a huge emotional impact on their willingness to accept your message and take the desired action. If they get the impression that you are sincere, focused on them (rather than on yourself), and confident in your subject matter, they are much more likely to buy into your presentation than if they see you as unsure of your actions, timid, and only concerned with yourself. That means that the examples you use, the choices you make about terminology, and whether you sound like you understand your audience carry great weight.

Verbal factors to consider include the following:

◆ **Use real examples**. If you want members of your audience to recognize that you understand their situation, the examples you use must relate to their world. If audience members are the end users of your software, don't tell them "it's an easy-to-use interface for database searches." Try using their examples. "Are you tired of taking forever to find out who hasn't completed their paperwork yet? Here's how easy it is . . . ."

STEP 7

◆ **Use "apples to apples" comparisons.** You want to convince members of your audience that what you're asking them to do (whether learn a skill or buy your software) is going to make their life easier and applies to them. For that reason, make sure that the examples you use relate to that audience. If, for example, your audience is made up of small business owners, bragging about how IBM uses your stuff might have the wrong impact; they might think of you as too complicated or expensive. If you have a small business audience, use small business examples. If you're teaching individual contributors to process their paperwork correctly, use an example from their world.

◆ **Keep success stories and examples short and sweet.** Bragging or getting carried away with your examples is easy. Some people present as if they believe that quantity of evidence beats quality. In fact, short, focused examples work best. If the audience wants more, members will ask for it during the question-and-answer period. Write your success stories out and practice them so you're not tempted to go freestyle and ramble. A good example or success story contains three components:

- **The situation.** "We had a client like you who was struggling with_____."
- **The solution.** "We used our patented consulting process to discover the client's biggest issue was _____."
- **The result.** "As a result, we didn't have to spend a lot of time and money on other things; we just focused on _____ and got the client back up and running in less than a week, and we saved the client thousands of dollars."

◆ **Don't use jargon or acronyms.** Unless members of your audience know as much about your topic as you do, be careful of using terminology or acronyms that might throw them off. What sounds to you like expertise can come across to your audience as condescending or off-putting. If participants don't know what you're saying, they'll find it hard to buy in. If you do use an acronym, always explain it the first time you use it, and putting it on a visual so people can read it also helps. In addition, use audience members' terminology if possible. If you call employees "associates" and they call them "cast members," as they do at Disney, change your terminology accordingly.

◆ **Avoid repetitive language and "comfort words."** Over time presenters develop habits that might go unnoticed by them but are picked up by their audience. One of the most common involves using the same word over and over (often in place of the dreaded *um*). For example, I'm notorious for inserting the word *now* before a new thought or idea. *Basically* is another common culprit. Get honest feedback during rehearsal on your comfort language and terms before you drive your audience crazy.

◆ **Use participant names.** People respond automatically when they hear their names mentioned. Even if they have started to drift off or have gone to email land, if you use examples including their names ("Let's say that Jeanie has a customer with a delivery problem"), people will automatically reconnect.

Tips for Vocal Excellence

The tone and quality of your voice can make it comfortable for audience members to listen to and keep them engaged—or make it difficult for them to listen to, which will shorten their attention span. A good voice has plenty of energy, speaks neither too quickly nor too slowly, and uses few "fillers."

Keeping the Energy Level Up

◆ **Volume is the key**. Being interesting is almost impossible when speaking in a quiet, whispering tone. Yet many people seem more concerned about their officemates or the person in the next cubicle than about their audience. Speak at the same volume you would use in a meeting where your voice has to project to the end of the conference table.

◆ **Don't look at the monitor.** Your voice tends to follow your eyes. Consider being on the phone with someone and whether or not you can tell when he or she is hunting for a piece of information. Your audience is just as observant as you are. When you forget you're talking to an audience and simply talk to the monitor, your voice will get quieter, first because your voice is overruled by your eyes and you wouldn't naturally shout at something only a few inches away, and second because your brain tells you that the computer is an inanimate object. Look over your monitor and imagine the faces of the people you're speaking to. I pick three different spots on the wall and present to those spots as if they are live participants.

◆ **Keep your hands free to drive—and to gesture.** Even though in most cases the audience can't see you for most of your presentation, you want to gesture and use your hands when you speak. This will keep the energy level in your voice high, and your audience will be able to tell. Use a headset if at all possible, or at least a good speakerphone (if you're dialing in by telephone) and a quiet room. Don't worry about what the people sitting around you think—your concern is your audience, not the fellow residents of your cubicle farm.

Watch the Speed and Inflection in Your Voice

◆ **Don't be afraid to pause.** One inevitable result of not being able to see your audience is the tendency to speak more quickly than you ought to, which occurs because you're not getting the nonverbal cues that tell you to slow the heck down. Whether you're transitioning between slides, using the annotation tools, or just changing thoughts, know that the pause sounds infinitely longer to you than it does to your audience.

◆ **Speak to your audience; don't present.** When you present to an audience, you can sound stilted and unnatural. When you just speak to people, however, you sound

STEP **7**

natural and relaxed. Try a bit of a mental exercise: Don't imagine yourself giving a big formal lecture; imagine the other people seated across the table from you and speak naturally.

◆ **Use professional but informal language whenever appropriate.** Unless they have a compelling reason not to, most people prefer to listen to natural-sounding language as opposed to very formal speech. The more natural you sound, the fewer barriers people will put up to your message. You shouldn't be unprofessional or use inappropriate language, but don't try to sound smarter than your audience either. Using language you wouldn't ordinarily use is a recipe for tripping yourself up and forgetting words.

◆ **Don't try to get everything letter-perfect.** One of the most surprising findings in my work with clients is that people care more about the humanity of the speaker than the perfection of the speech. Getting every word precisely right and never tripping up actually can sound robotic to the audience, and the quest for perfection can really mess with your head. Relax: The audience doesn't mind an occasional missed word or mispronunciation. Just apologize, laugh it off, and move on—the audience will.

◆ **Don't read to your audience.** Nobody over the age of eight likes being read to. Many presenters presume that because they want to get the information correct and the audience can't see them, they can simply read their presentation. You might get all the information correct, but members of your audience will roll their eyes and tune out. Unless something has to be said exactly word for word (for example, you're quoting something or someone), just use bullet points and rehearse until you know your content.

◆ **This goes double for the words in PowerPoint.** Putting a whole bunch of information on a PowerPoint slide is problematic. Then turning around and reading it word for word to your audience simply compounds the pain for everyone. Either keep the bullets short enough that you only use key words, or paraphrase the bullets so you don't simply parrot what's on the screen.

◆ **Finish your sentences on a high note.** Many presenters do well throughout their paragraph or thought but as they reach the end trail off because they don't know quite how to finish, or they're already thinking about moving to the next slide. As a result, the audience hears your voice trail off, which sounds less than confident and certainly not engaging. Imagine finishing your sentence locked eye-to-eye with your audience, and don't worry about switching slides until you need to switch slides.

◆ **Make declarative sentences.** One common challenge for new presenters and those unsure of themselves no matter how long they've been at it is making statements that sound like questions. Their voice trails up at the end as if seeking reassurance from the audience. Often they end those sentences with "right?" or "OK?" You know your material. Make your statement and keep your voice as firm and confident at the end of your sentence or thought as at the beginning.

Controlling the Dreaded Ums

◆ **Pause. Just pause.** Human beings fear pauses in conversation. People might sound like they don't know what they're saying, or someone might jump in and interrupt them. The fact is that time is relative (Einstein once said that a second with your hand on a hot stove feels like an hour, and an hour with a pretty girl feels like a second—and he should know about relativity). Pauses feel much longer to the speaker than they do to the audience. When you've said what you have to say, stop talking, visualize the first word of the next sentence, and start cleanly with that word.

◆ **Don't move the mouse and speak at the same time.** Despite what it says on your résumé, you don't multitask very well. Moving the mouse during a demo, say, advancing the slides on your web presentation, and focusing on what you're saying is very difficult. Pause; click; resume.

◆ **Break your script or notes into small chunks.** One of the most common reasons even good speakers sometimes have to fill dead air is that they lose their place in their notes and have to look for their next point. If you have a script, don't write it out in big paragraphs. You'll eventually lose your place and have to hunt through it to find where you left off. Visually break it into bullet points and have lots of white space on your page so you can easily find the information you need.

◆ **Take a break by letting others speak.** If you speak for a long time without feedback or a break, your brain will demand time out. Make your meeting or presentation more conversational than presentation style if possible. You can do this in several different ways:

• Allow participants to participate vocally (unmute individual phones so people can ask questions or comment if your platform allows this).

• Call on other presentation participants who are subject matter experts to give people another voice to hear and back up your own credibility on a topic ("Joanne, you were at that meeting. What did you think?").

• Set up your presentation as an interview or a series of interviews, like having your own radio talk show. This not only presents a great way to build your own credibility by bringing experts to your audience, but people perk up whenever they hear a change in speakers. It also frees you from doing all the work, which isn't a bad thing either.

◆ **Practice with the tool so you get comfortable.** Being aware of what you're doing as a presenter is impossible if your brain is in a panic about which button to push and whether your audience can see your presentation properly. By getting comfortable with the presentation platform, you free up the mental bandwidth to concentrate on your content.

STEP **7**

Interact With Your Audience to Get That "Live Presentation" Feeling

This book has consistently shown you that while presenting online doesn't give you the same adrenaline rush (which is what you call it if you like it; you call it "stage fright" if you don't) as speaking in front of a roomful of human beings, accomplishing your objectives is still possible.

With a little practice, you can become one of a depressingly small group of people: effective, engaging web presenters.

Most web presenters don't accomplish this for a simple reason: Either they don't know what's possible (you no longer have that excuse) or, in the heat of actually presenting, they focus so intently on delivering the information that they completely forget about the audience.

The easiest way to create interaction is to know how to get feedback using whichever platform you use, and then build interaction into your presentation so that you can't possibly forget it.

Consider the following ways to build live audience feedback into your presentation:

◆ **You can't forget it if it's built into your slide deck.** If you plan to ask the audience a question, create a slide in your deck to cue yourself and the audience. Write the question out, and then let people know how you want them to answer it, whether by chat, chiming in vocally, or using the "raise hand" button.

◆ **Make sure you have your slides printed out beside you with cues, and track yourself as you go.** Experienced presenters tend to ignore the script or facilitator's guide once they've learned a program. I find it helpful to have the printed "Notes" outline with me. On each page that requires interaction, I include a simple note like "Check in here," if I'm checking for buy-in or that people are paying attention.

- **If your platform has an attendance meter, use it for its intended purpose.** Some of the more robust platforms, especially those built for training purposes (for example, GoToTraining, some WebEx versions, and Adobe Connect), have a meter on the leader's toolbar that measures attention. This basically means that the server can tell if someone has opened another window on his or her computer and is running your presentation in the background. Think of this as the online version of looking at your audience members and seeing them all typing on their BlackBerrys instead of listening to you. Nine times out of 10 this means they're checking email. If you notice attention dropping, take time to answer questions or ask for participants' input via chat. This tool is designed to give guidance to the presenter, not punish the audience. Try not to call attention to the fact that people are not paying attention—it seems a bit dictatorial, and they will know you're spying on them.

- **Play fair with your audience: Don't spring interaction on people halfway through.** If you want your audience to be participative and engaged, you can't lull them to sleep and then bring them back—at least not very effectively. Use the planning tools and formats discussed in this book to engage them early and often. Set the expectation of their participation, and asking them for input won't catch them by surprise.

- **Give very clear directions so they don't freak out.** If you've ever been in a meeting or training session where the leader gives a whole bunch of directions and then has to repeat them multiple times, you know this feeling. Now multiply it by the effect of using unfamiliar or uncomfortable technology, and you can't see the panicky look on audience members' faces. When you give the audience instructions, do it one step at a time, and don't leave folks behind. Reinforce the instructions with a written PowerPoint slide if that helps. Here's an example of how to call for written feedback using chat:

> "OK, I want you to use the chat feature to answer this question for me: 'What's the most difficult part of managing a remote team?' Does everyone know where the chat feature is? OK, type your answer now, and we'll see what you come up with."

Something That Will Help

The hardest part about improving your presentation skills is being objective about what the audience sees and hears. Improvement requires constant feedback, practice, and more feedback to reinforce your strengths as a presenter and identify areas in need of improvement.

Take every opportunity to get feedback on your online presentations. If no one is around, record your webinars and online presentations. You can always delete them later, but you'll have a chance to see and hear everything the audience does. Consider this the equivalent of videotaping your presentations—every bit as painful and invaluable.

Have a partner or someone you trust use the verbal and vocal skills checklist provided in Worksheet 7.1 to give you the good behavioral feedback you need to improve.

Wrap-Up

Face it: Virtual presentations are a different animal than you've dealt with before. Simple things that happen naturally in a face-to-face setting—like seeing the faces of audience members and sending or receiving nonverbal signals—happen in an unusual way online. Don't be too frustrated if your years of experience haven't prepared you for this: Never before in human history have professionals had to present virtually. You are entering uncharted waters.

A great virtual presentation does more than simply send information over the wire from one person to another. When you present effectively, you elevate simple data transfer to true communication.

For experienced presenters, you'll be out of your comfort zone at first, but eventually you'll become comfortable enough for your instincts to take over, and you'll find that presenting online is very similar to what you already know. If you don't enjoy presenting, at least know that you will become competent if you do it often enough, just as with any skill.

Cut yourself some slack, breathe, and give yourself a chance to continually improve. With practice, you will become every bit as confident and successful presenting online as at the front of the room—maybe more so, because you can wear your bunny slippers and sit in your comfiest chair if you want to. A relaxed, confident delivery will get you that much closer to your objectives.

The trick is to
- ◆ make what the audience sees appear smooth and professional
- ◆ make what the audience hears engaging and effective
- ◆ interact with the audience to get that "live presentation" feeling.

STEP **7**

WORKSHEET 7.1
Verbal and Vocal Skills Checklist

This checklist has many purposes. You can ask trusted team members for feedback during rehearsal, or you can have someone monitor you during the actual presentation itself. Perhaps more important, if you record your web presentations and webinars, you can experience the presentation as your audience does.

Whether for a boss, a co-worker, a trusted audience member, or yourself, the key here is to offer specific, behavioral feedback. Each section includes room for written comments. If a real example was not good, explain why not. Perhaps it addressed an issue your audience couldn't relate to, or maybe it was too technical. If at some point you sounded distracted and the *ums* and *ers* showed up, remember exactly where. If you can identify what happened, you can fix it next time.

And there *will* be a next time.

Verbal Skills

What You Heard	Needs Improvement	Meets Expectations	Excellent
Uses real examples			
Success stories are clear and concise			
Doesn't use jargon or acronyms			
Avoids repetitive or "comfort" words			
Uses participant names			
Uses appropriate language			

Vocal Skills

What You Heard	Needs Improvement	Meets Expectations	Excellent
Speaks at a clear volume			
Voice sounds energetic and interesting			
Speed is not too fast			
Pauses are frequent and comfortable			
Doesn't obviously read to the audience			

STEP 7

Worksheet 7.1, continued

What You Heard	Needs Improvement	Meets Expectations	Excellent
Finishes sentences on a positive note			
Doesn't use *ums* or fillers			

Interaction

What You Heard	Needs Improvement	Meets Expectations	Excellent
Instructions are clear and easy to follow			
There were no dead spots where the audience felt disengaged			
The activities or questions made sense to the audience members			
Presenter sounded confident and interested in the audience			
Working with the chat and other technology appeared seamless to the audience			

STEP 7

STEP
7

Rehearse

O V E R V I E W

Conduct a first and
second rehearsal

Monitor rehearsal activity

Ask for feedback

Many of you readers are experienced live presenters who feel fairly comfortable with your material and being in front of a crowd. As a result, you might not feel the need to rehearse very often. Maybe you repeat the same material, or you always work with the same people with whom you feel comfortable communicating.

When it comes to presenting online, though, the added complexity of using the media prevents reliance on an old skill set (at least until you get comfortable with the new material and tools).

Let's be clear: Rehearsal does not mean flipping through your PowerPoint visuals while muttering to yourself. True rehearsal means going through the entire presentation from log-in to sign-off. Everyone involved in the presentation (the producer and any co-presenters) should participate in the rehearsal as well.

You should rehearse for multiple reasons:
◆ You want to make sure you appear comfortable and competent using the technology.

S T E P **8**

If you absolutely can't get someone else to join you for rehearsal, use the record feature. Record your presentation and play it back, using the tools and job aids to make careful notes. Be as objective as you can, trying to put yourself in the shoes (or desk chair, as the case may be) of your intended audience.

◆ You want to make sure your message is clear and you support your objectives.

◆ If working with a co-presenter, you want to make sure the transitions and handoffs are smooth and that you work together effectively.

To be objective about your own presentation is impossible. Of course your pace sounds good and your objective is clear. Staring at and editing your own PowerPoint slides for a long enough time will keep you from seeing even the most obvious typos (I know what I'm talking about—I recently misspelled the word *assess* in the most embarrassing way possible in front of a major prospect). Get at least one other person's opinion whenever possible. The job aid and checklist in this section will help you get good feedback from even inexperienced partners. Your goal is to get specific, behavior-focused feedback that will tighten your presentation and increase the odds of accomplishing your objectives.

Conduct a First and Second Rehearsal

You should have two rehearsals, each a few days apart. The first rehearsal is to check content issues and ensure everything flows and makes sense. The second rehearsal is more of a true dress rehearsal, where you'll fine-tune your presentation skills and ensure you're completely comfortable with all of the moving parts.

To determine how much rehearsal time you need, think about the extent of your familiarity with the material and your comfort with the technology platform. Give yourself more time when the stakes are high or the material is complex (a new training course or a critical marketing webinar).

Ideally, hold the first rehearsal a full week before the actual live presentation for a simple reason: to check for content and to see if your presentation runs for the correct length of time. If you have to make any drastic changes to your visuals or your content, you don't want to be burning the midnight oil the night before your presentation. Make it easy on yourself.

Hold the second rehearsal 48 hours before the event. That will give you enough time to fix any last-minute issues that may pop up.

Monitor Rehearsal Activity

Ask yourself the following four questions during rehearsal—particularly the first rehearsal:

◆ What's the audience experience?
◆ Does the presentation look and sound like you envisioned it?
◆ Do you look and sound professional and competent while delivering your material and using the technology?
◆ Are you moving toward your objective?

STEP **8**

What's the Audience Experience?

No matter how compelling your content, and no matter how slickly you use all the cool features of a web presentation, if members of your audience don't have a good experience, you will have difficulty getting them to take action. If having to log in multiple times makes them cranky or they can't hear properly, they won't be disposed to like you or your message. For this reason your rehearsal should mimic the real circumstances of the presentation as closely as possible. This helps you catch any potential annoyances in a safe environment.

You want your rehearsal partner(s) to experience and comment on the ease of logging on and signing in, the power of your presentation, the quality of your delivery, and the clarity of your message.

Log-on and sign-in. Make it easy and stress-free for your audience to get into your web presentation and take part. You cannot present effectively if people can't see or hear the presentation. Have your rehearsal partner or coach log in the same way you expect your audience to arrive:

◆ If you've sent participants a link, have your partner log in via the same kind of link. This way you'll know if broken links cause a problem or if a firewall gets in the way.

◆ Many of the best tools—GoToMeeting, Dimdim, and especially WebEx and Live Meeting—include computer system tests and audio tests. Have your partner run those tests on his or her computer, and put instructions or the link (depending on the platform) in the invitation. Chances are participants won't take advantage of the opportunity, but you've done what you can for them.

◆ If at all possible, have your partner log on from somewhere other than behind your own firewall. If members of your audience will be in a remote location (which is likely or you could just call them into the conference room) and on a different network, they will be at the mercy of different network security settings and defaults. You don't want someone's paranoid IT people ruining your presentation by installing pop-up blockers or other settings.

◆ Have your partner connect to the audio in the way your audience will. If audience members will use the audio provided by the computer platform provider, then your partner should use a microphone and headset. If participants will dial in using a particular conference provider, then your partner should dial in using the same one. Don't let convenience or cost stop you from testing every possible variable.

Does the Presentation Look and Sound Like You Envisioned It?

What the audience sees, along with what the audience hears, will determine the power of your presentation.

◆ Do the colors, formatting, and templates look as good on your audience's computers as they do on yours? Standard PowerPoint templates usually transfer to the online environment just fine. But if you are using a custom template or the latest version of your presentation software, the platform may create unexpected havoc by washing out certain backgrounds, mysteriously moving pictures, and scrambling some of your letters or symbols. One of the great frustrations of web presenting is that something can look good on your computer but not on others. This gets complicated when dealing with attendees on slower computers or outside of your internal network.

◆ Double check your spelling and grammar. It often takes more than one set of eyes to catch spelling errors (the most common are homonyms like *their, they're*, and *there*, which spell-check won't catch).

◆ Check your webcam resolution. Video that looks great on a fast T-1 line (your usual office network; it's faster than a home DSL line, racing along at 1.4 megabytes per second) in the office can look choppy and distorted on the network at your local coffee shop's wifi. Often you'll decide against using webcams or limit their use, based on what your audience experiences in rehearsal. Also, check your background and free it of distractions. Use good eye contact.

STEP 8

◆ Make sure the features work correctly. Such tools as whiteboards and polling are wonderful additions to your presentation—but only if they work. Get your partner to actually do whatever you will ask your audience to do. If audience members will vote using polling, actually poll your rehearsal partner. If you want people to write on the whiteboard, have your partner practice that too.

◆ When using annotation tools such as highlighting, move them confidently in smooth motions. Make sure you are able to switch seamlessly between using the various tools.

◆ Don't spend too much time on a visual that doesn't change. This might lose your audience. Ask your coach to give you some guidance on whether you need to add another visual in a particular section of your presentation or augment it by using annotation tools or animation.

◆ Check the lag time. During rehearsal, especially if you are just testing the features before you begin rehearsing the presentation itself, check in frequently with your audience. "You should be seeing _____ now," for example. When you use the annotation tools, note whether the colored highlighting appears instantly or takes a second or two. Understanding the lag time allows you to prevent panicky comments and confusion from your audience.

◆ Evaluate your graphics for clarity. Your graphs and charts should be clear and concise, but when you've worked on them for days on end, they might make more sense to you than to an uninitiated audience. Ask for honest feedback—for example, whether the axes are clearly labeled and whether the colors look good. Solicit this feedback while you still have plenty of time to make any changes.

Every bit as important as what it sees is **what the audience hears**:

◆ Make your opening statement confident and concise. Remember to write it out so that you can say it confidently and without error and then deliver it without sounding like you're reading it verbatim.

◆ Smooth out your transitions. Finish your sentences with as much energy as you start them. When making a statement, don't raise your voice at the end so it becomes a question. Remember, writing your transitions out and keeping them where you can see them will help a great deal.

◆ Avoid using the same transition statements all the time. Remember to vary the transitions and use this time to let audience members ask questions, check in with them, and process the valuable information you've just imparted to them.

◆ Avoid using lots of *ums* and *ers*. Because your audience relies on your voice for so much of the impact online, these little habits (which can be ignored or overcome in a face-to-face meeting) become much more important online. Have your coach count them and note where they occur (odds are it's either just before or just after you move from one visual to another).

◆ Try not to sound as if you're reading word for word. This drives audiences crazy over long periods of time.

◆ Make sure your voice rises and falls as it would in normal conversation rather than projecting in a monotone.

◆ Check in with your audience members and engage them instead of just talking to them. Remember to interact with your audience every four to five visuals.

◆ Monitor your rate of speech. Don't speak too fast or too slow, and be deliberate.

Does the Content Make Sense to the Audience?

◆ Does your introduction answer the big three questions (what are they doing there, what's in it for them, and how long will it take?) that members of your audience really need to know?

STEP **8**

- Are you using relevant examples that the audience for this specific presentation can relate to?
- Are you using jargon, acronyms, and terminology your audience might not be familiar with?
- Is the level of detail appropriate to the audience? Too much can overwhelm people; not enough can cost you credibility.
- How are you doing with hitting your time milestones? Your coach should be using the tool in Worksheet 8.1 to give you an accurate picture of where you're spending your time—where you're getting bogged down or where you could add more detail and examples.
- Can the people you're rehearsing with clearly state the call to action? Is it clear to them?

Are You Moving Toward Your Objective?

- Is the call to action obvious? Do participants know exactly what they are supposed to do?
- Does the audience for your rehearsal feel you made your case? Are the examples compelling? Is your evidence sufficient to overcome objections?
- Does the audience have objections that haven't occurred to you? Better to raise them now and build them into your edited script than be surprised by an unexpected question.

Ask for Feedback

The whole purpose of rehearsal is to identify the strengths and weaknesses of your presentation—and to strengthen the latter. To do this, seek feedback that is behavior based, clear, and aimed at helping you reach your objectives.

The tools included in this book will certainly help your rehearsal partners provide that type of feedback, but make sure you explain exactly what you're looking for.

Behavior-based feedback involves something an audience member specifically saw or heard. "That was great" isn't helpful. "I really like the way you used the highlighter to check off the points one by one" is a behavior you can reinforce. Make sure people are specific about what they saw or heard that they liked or didn't.

Specific feedback is also important. "I didn't like the way you explained your value proposition" doesn't help. "You're spending too much time explaining your value proposition. Try boiling it down to a single sentence" is clear.

Finally, audience members need to know your goals for the presentation so they can help you achieve them. Your audience should know

♦ your expected outcomes
♦ how long you expect your presentation to run.

> **POINTER**
>
> To make the rehearsal feedback tools easier to use, number your slides so that the numbers are visible to the audience. This practice is not recommended during the final presentation, but for rehearsal it facilitates being specific. For example, "On slide 4 your graph isn't labeled clearly—make sure we know that you're measuring rainfall in inches, not centimeters."

Worksheet 8.1 is great for getting this specific feedback.

One thing to watch for: Time can be measured in one of two ways—running time (starting at 0:00 and counting up) or real time (starting at 1:05, for example, and then following the time on your computer clock for measurement)—depending on your preference.

Wrap-Up

Whether you do two rehearsals for new material or just one because you're familiar with the content and the platform, the more feedback you get, the better. Remember that presenting comes from muscle memory—the more you practice, the more natural and less stressful the action will feel.

When rehearsing, ask yourself the following questions:

◆ What is the audience experience?

◆ Does the presentation look and sound like you envisioned it? If not, you still have time to fix things.

◆ Do you look and sound professional and competent while delivering your material and using the technology?

◆ Is it moving you toward your objective? After all, you put yourself through all this to reach your goal.

WORKSHEET 8.1

Rehearsal Feedback

Send this tool in advance to everyone sitting in on your rehearsal so these participants can make timely, specific comments. A PDF form is fine, although if you send it in Word or as a template so they can type as they go, you may get more quality input.

Writing specific, actionable comments down as you see and hear them is so much easier than trying to remember what the speaker said after the fact.

As the speaker, you should record each rehearsal session and make notes for yourself as well.

Visual	What You See	What You Hear	Impact on Outcome	Time

STEP 8

STEP 8

Present and Multitask Effectively

Prepare yourself to be relaxed and confident

Multitask without making yourself crazy

Use question-and-answer time effectively

Close your presentation to meet your objectives

Now's the time to put together everything you have planned. Plenty of chaos will be going on in your head, but you know you'll be at your best if you relax and project yourself with confidence.

Prepare Yourself to Be Relaxed and Confident

Presenters make several mistakes that make things more difficult than necessary. Most stem from the same core problem: not logging on early enough to get set up. If you log on too close to showtime, you'll feel rushed and likely forget something important. The single most important tip of this whole section is this:

Give yourself plenty of time to get set up. Half an hour before the start time is a minimum.

Try the following setup tips to help create a more relaxed environment:

◆ Put your script in a three-ring binder and stand it up beside your computer where you can see it.

STEP 9

- Check your webcam for angle and distractions. Nobody needs to see you jiggle your camera into position.
- Use a headset on your phone if possible. Only use a speakerphone if the quality is good and you are in a closed room, safe from interruption and background noise.
- Don't forget to annotate your slides to keep them interesting. Mark your script at appropriate places.
- Make sure you have a glass of water handy.
- Don't over-caffeinate yourself. Your brain is already pumping out enough adrenaline and cortisol to power a small city.
- Log on at least 30 minutes early to ensure good communication with your co-presenter.
- Unless you've created and stored them for retrieval, create or upload all polling questions immediately after setting up the meeting and test them to make sure they work.
- Test your slide advancement, annotation tools, and anything else you plan to use before the participants begin to arrive.
- Set your audio to "host and presenter" mode only. Whether you're using the platform's audio or teleconference, make sure the audience can't hear you talking to yourself or others—many presenters say things under stress that they don't want the audience to hear (trust me on this one).
- Make periodic announcements to your audience about exactly when you're going to start.

- If you're on a teleconference for audio, make sure you don't hear people "beeping in," especially with large audiences. It will drive you and the audience crazy.
- Attend to all biological needs eight to 10 minutes before showtime.

Use the checklist in Worksheet 9.1 to make sure you haven't forgotten any important steps along the way. This will give you peace of mind—you know you will be ready when the presentation begins.

Multitask Without Making Yourself Crazy

Before getting into the weeds on this subject, you need to know the problem with multitasking: It's impossible. You can't do it. Your brain doesn't work that way. That doesn't provide much comfort, but it helps to understand what's really going on: "serial processing." You're actually doing not three things at once but three different things, one after the other in rapid sequence. To process serially, you need to know what you're doing, in what sequence, and give yourself permission to do all those steps calmly and in a way that looks professional and controlled to your audience.

Presenting has a rhythm, and you should recognize it by now:
1. speak
2. pause
3. prepare
4. act
5. speak again.

While it might seem time consuming, in fact it only takes a second to scan the chat function for new input or type something on a whiteboard. The audience will not notice the pause. In fact, because it slows you down and gives audience members a chance to process the information, they will probably appreciate it.

STEP **9**

WORKSHEET 9.1

Show-Day Checklist

All program-day participants should receive a copy of this checklist so that they know what is involved and has to happen. Final responsibility of distributing this rests with the producer.

If it seems like overkill, remember that pilots go over a checklist whenever they get into the cockpit, no matter how many hours of flying time they have. Feel better now?

Time	Task	Done?
30 minutes prior	Log in to meeting	
30 minutes prior	Ensure telephony is working and recording functional	
30 minutes prior	Upload and run "cycle slides" (if applicable)	
20 minutes prior	Ensure polling slides are created and loaded properly	
20 minutes prior	Check that other visuals or applications as necessary are ready to go	
15 minutes prior	Make a 15-minute announcement	
10 minutes prior	Make a 10-minute announcement	
5 minutes priors	Make a 5-minute announcement	
1 minute prior	Hit "record"	
Showtime!	Introduce webinar	
	Deliver your presentation	
	Monitor time	
	Monitor question-and-answer box, choose questions, and answer the easy ones	
	Introduce question-and-answer	
	Check for audience questions, and use prepared or planted questions to jump-start the session if necessary	
	Close presentation	
	Turn off recording	
	Copy question-and-answer log (if appropriate) to the platform	
	Save presentation with polling data and annotations (if appropriate) to the platform	
5 minutes after	Close the platform; end the webinar	

STEP **9**

Let's take a couple of common examples and apply this rhythm to them.

Suppose you are moving between visuals and not doing anything more dramatic than that. It should sound and look like this:

YOU: And that's why we need to always use the 17B form when requesting extra resources.

[Pause.]

[Click the advance arrow to make sure the next slide appears. When you are sure what you want to say next, continue.]

YOU: Once you've made the request, it's important to remember that . . .

Easy, right? If you have people chatting to you now, follow the same process:

YOU: And so now that we've seen how raising cockatiels can lower your blood pressure, let's see how they compare to other pets . . .

[Pause.]

[Advance the slide.]

[Scan the chat box. You have new comments.]

YOU: We've had a couple of people make comments in the chat box—thank you for that.

[Pause.]

[Read the chats, and choose any you want to comment on.]

YOU: Wow, Paul, that's a great comment—did everyone read that?

[Repeat the comment to the group.]

A couple of interesting dynamics are at work when you follow these steps:

◆ If you do this periodically throughout your presentation, you won't get overwhelmed with new comments or questions. You can quickly scan for new information.

◆ If you say, "I'm going to check the chat real quickly" and pause, your audience will do the same thing. This not only keeps participants busy during the momentary pauses but actually encourages them to contribute with comments or additional questions.

◆ By truly pausing, the audience won't hear you muttering, and you won't feel the need to fill the silence with *ums*.

This same rhythm applies when you use your annotation tools, share applications, or do almost anything else. As you get more comfortable, the rhythm becomes more fluid and seamless to the audience.

Some additional pointers for doing multiple tasks efficiently are the following:

◆ **Remember to listen.** Whether you're training, doing a webinar, or conducting a sales call with a client, you have to listen when people speak. You can't do that effectively while searching for your highlighter or reading questions. Really pause and listen to the other person. Repeat the question or rephrase what he or she has said to show understanding. That bright green line you were going to put on the screen can wait.

◆ **Don't rush.** Your audience typically won't notice that small pause that seems like an eternity to you. Your participants would rather you pause and move purposefully than stumble around.

◆ **Communicate.** To eliminate the fear of losing members of your audience while you're performing a task, tell them exactly what you're doing and that it might take a moment. For example, at the beginning of many webinar classes, I tell the participants I'm going to turn off my webcam (in the interest of saving their bandwidth) and that it might take a moment for them to see it on their screens. I click off my camera, check my notes, and then begin on the next visual.

◆ **Alert the audience to changes.** Remember that your audience might be less familiar with web-based presentations than you are, and people may get mildly stressed if unexpected things happen (even those things you've carefully planned for effect). Tell them what is about to happen, make it happen, and check in to confirm that they see what you intend. The results are well worth the second or two of silence. It will prevent a series of panicky, "I've just lost the video feed" chat messages.

Use Question-and-Answer Time Effectively

During the bulk of your presentation, you control the flow of information. You can say what you want to say, how you want to say it. Because of that feeling of control, many presenters fear the question-and-answer session. After all, they might not know the answer to a question, or someone might be "gunning for them" and make them appear unconfident. As a result, many presenters treat it as a necessary evil rather than an integral part of the presentation.

The question-and-answer period can help you do the following:

◆ **Eliminate distractions from the minds of your audience.** Very often an audience member has a concern (such as the time it might take to learn a new software program) that will make it almost impossible for him or her to hear anything else you say. By letting this person ask a question, and then putting his or her mind at ease, you have made him or her feel better and moved closer to your objective. Answering an audience member's question and thereby relieving his or her stress is better than just letting it sit there like "the elephant in the room."

◆ **Clear up bad information.** Just as in sales, audience objections to your plans are often based on bad information. "We already tried this, and it didn't work" is a common comment. Take this chance to say how your suggestion differs from what people tried before, or how what you have learned will ensure different results. Maybe audience members have a false belief, such as "web training never works," based on past experience or a lack of knowledge of how much has changed. Either way, you want to give them

STEP 9

new, better information that will help eliminate barriers to their learning or buy-in.

◆ **Repeat your message in a new way.** You have chosen your words for this presentation very carefully, but audience members will not necessarily understand what you say the first time. Maybe they aren't familiar with the example you used or they were off answering email. You want to have every opportunity to get your message across, so grab the opportunity to correct anything you may have said incorrectly or at least not as clearly as you thought you had the first time.

◆ **Get buy-in and move toward your objective.** Put at its most basic, people are social animals, and they tend to follow a herd mentality. If the rest of the group tends to lean in one direction, most people will go along. A question-and-answer period allows you to test the waters and help move people to adopt your suggestion or buy your product. Many questions come from people imagining the outcome—for example, "If we go with this, would it take long to learn?" They are already trying to see what it would look like, so you just need to reinforce the positives.

Look at the question portion of your presentation as the final step to nailing your objective. Eliminate questions and objections that might stop people from taking the action steps you need, reinforce your message, and build on the momentum you've developed.

Whether you let people ask questions by voice or just take them via the chat window, follow these tips for making the best of this opportunity:

Repeat the question. A best practice is to always repeat the question (in chat you might have to decipher the questioner's spelling or intent), for two reasons. The first is practical: Because of different audio connections (or they were just daydreaming), a lot of people may not have heard the question in the first place. Let them hear the question before you answer it. Second, by simply repeating the question, you give your own brain a chance to think about the answer before just blurting out the first thing that occurs to you.

Eliminate negative language. Sometimes you want to rephrase the question. "Whose idiotic idea was this?" is not exactly how you want to position your answer (especially when the idiot in question is you). What participants really want to know is, "Where did this idea come from?"—a much easier and much less threatening question to answer. Remember, when your jaw clenches, your voice reflects it. Smile and stay positive.

Go slow. Many presenters have a natural inclination to answer the question as quickly as possible, because that makes them look prepared and very, very smart. But presenters don't necessarily look smart when they don't answer the question the person actually asked, or give too much information and start a barrage of questions that are off-topic or counterproductive. Take your time and answer correctly the first time.

Pause and start on the first word of your answer. Fair or not, any answer that starts with *uh* is going to be suspect. Take a pause, imagine the first word of your answer, and start there. Don't fear the pause. What feels to you like fumbling for an answer might actually seem to your audience like giving thought to the answer.

Finish your answer by tying back to your outcome. Many presenters fall into the trap of answering questions for their own sake. Remember that every answer you give, and every part of your presentation until you sign off, is designed to do one thing: move your audience toward taking your desired action. Whether your presentation involves training, processing information, or demonstrating a product, the answers you give should always move you closer to your goal. The easiest way to do this is to use some simple phrases at the end of your answer:
- "So that's why this information is important, because when you use this process . . . ."

- "What that means to you back on the job is . . . ."
- "Of course, in your particular example, that will help you . . . ."

Test buy-in. After you have answered a question, check with the person who asked it. You want to make sure he or she understands the answer. Also gauge his or her buy-in. Questions like, "Does that make you more likely to use this product?" and "Is there anything else that might get in the way of your using this product?" give people an opportunity to raise other concerns, or, if your answers satisfy them, it will signal to the rest of the audience that people are buying in to your ideas.

Close Your Presentation to Meet Your Objectives

Imagine yourself running a race. Ahead of the pack, you see the finish line. Do you want to stop and admire the view, or do you want to push yourself to complete the course in as strong a fashion as possible?

It surprises me how many people do the hard work of their presentation but don't complete the job in a way that moves the sale forward or ensures their audience learned anything.

Several things can derail your presentation at the end:
- You do not allow enough time for questions. People might not have the chance to clarify issues or be properly informed.
- Next steps aren't explicit. Don't assume people can see the next "logical" step.
- Your energy drops.
- The next step or call to action is difficult to convey.

This call to action is the reason you put yourself through the presentation process in the first place—the culmination of all your hard work and stress. To finish your presentation in as strong a fashion as you began it, try these tips:

◆ **Write out your call to action.** Practice saying it, and practice the way that you say it. Your call to action should answer any questions audience members may have about what you expect them to do. Keep crafting your call to action until it is a concise sentence or a couple of bullet points.

◆ **Put next steps on a visual.** Though not subtle, this works. Remember that people are more likely to retain information they see and hear. Having a PowerPoint slide or another visual that clearly outlines the next steps, including timelines, is always a good idea.

◆ **Be personal and specific.** People relate to personal pronouns and the use of their names or situations. Make sure you use lots of "we" and "you" language in your closing. "What I would like you to do is" carries less weight with the audience than "Here's what you should do next."

◆ **Make the next step automatic.** Many presentation platforms allow you to make the next step incredibly easy to take. Say your next action item is for people to subscribe to your newsletter. When you close the session in such platforms as WebEx and iLinc, you can actually have a webpage pop up with a link to your subscription site. If you want people to order your book, you can include a link to your website or to www.amazon.com. Even if you don't have one of these cool features, a simple thank-you email (covered in Step 10) should contain links so participants can take at least one action step in one click.

◆ **Provide contact information.** Members of your audience want to know that they'll have support and help if they do what you ask them to do. Make it easy for them to find you. A PowerPoint slide with your contact information is always a good idea—show it a couple of times. I often show mine both before I take questions (in case someone leaves early) and at the very end of the presentation.

◆ **Thank participants for their time and attention.** Unless you were raised by wolves, you will understand the benefit of politely thanking your audience members for their

STEP **9**

time—a precious commodity. They want to know you appreciate their efforts.

Wrap-Up

Prepare yourself to be relaxed and confident. Give yourself plenty of time, take advantage of your checklists to reduce stress, and take a big, deep breath. You are going to rock.

◆ Multitask without making yourself crazy. Remember that you're not really doing several things at once; you're just doing several things in rapid succession. Be deliberate, breathe, and plan what you'll do and when.

◆ Embrace the opportunity for question-and-answer time. Take your time, and consider this yet another opportunity to move closer to your objective. Enjoy it.

◆ Close your presentation to meet your objectives. If the audience leaves asking, "What am I supposed to do next?" your hard work has been largely for nothing. Avoid this type of criticism by closing your presentation just as strongly as you began it.

Follow Up and Keep Learning

Follow up to check your success

Capture best practices

Celebrate your accomplishments

You've finished your presentation; thanked your participants; and provided a concrete, concise call to action; however, you're not exactly done. Following up with your participants is an important final step to conducting a great virtual presentation.

Follow-up is important for two basic reasons:
◆ to confirm that you accomplished your goals (and, if you didn't, why)
◆ to capture feedback on what went well and what could have gone better.

Why start from scratch with every presentation when you have invested all this time and used all these planning tools? Presenting online, like any kind of presenting, involves both conscious thought and "muscle memory," your body's physical responses to stimuli based on past performance. If you've done something well, the more you practice it, the better you'll get at it. Many functions that have frustrated you in the past will become more and more natural to you, freeing you up to think about your content and your audience.

Similarly, a lot of the agonizing, slow, painstaking steps taken in this book are one-time functions. If you plan to present the same online webinar to another group, the settings, invitation process, and script or outline will remain essentially the same. By capturing this information, you can reduce the amount of work for next time without sacrificing the quality. Of course, if something didn't work well the first time, don't do that again.

This also makes it easy to help change the presentation culture where you work. Are your peers and colleagues as good at this as you are? Wouldn't it be great if, after all your hard work, you now had a set of best practices that anyone in your company could follow?

Enough with the rhetorical questions. Quality control and continuous improvement are parts of professionals' daily work lives, and giving great web presentations is no different. Remember that feedback is a gift, even if it feels like anything but.

This book has looked at four different types of presentations, and evaluation and follow-up will vary for each one, though the tools will overlap:

◆ **General town hall meetings and webinars.** You want to know about the audience's experience and the outcomes. Did participants enjoy the webinar? Were they bored? Could they easily log on and use the features? Then, of course, you need to learn their major takeaways: whether they understood the message and have acted on it.

◆ **Sales demos.** At the end of the day, your vice president of sales will have only one question for you after the presentation: Did you sell something (or at least move the customer to the next step of the sales cycle, such as a trial of your software)?

◆ **Training.** The only reason to put people through training is to teach them to actually do something differently or better. Essentially, you want to measure the audience experience and what people have done with the information back on the job. Be as in-depth as you think is appropriate.

◆ **Marketing webinars.** Marketing webinars are designed to bring people into your sales cycle and push them to the next level. Effective follow-up can achieve what is impossible for a live presentation—getting people who didn't attend to learn about your product or service. Follow-up should include both accounted-for attendees and people who registered but failed to show up. (Remember, marketing webinars have a 50 percent no-show rate, so this is important!)

POINTER

Don't discount the people who said they would attend and didn't. Industry studies show that four to 10 times more people will view the recorded version of a marketing webinar than will view the actual live event. Believe it or not, this is good news. Don't forget to record and post your presentations whenever possible!

Follow Up to Check Your Success

Great web presentations accomplish their goals. Follow-up checks to see if that happened. You will want to follow up with both people who attended the presentation and those who signed up but did not attend. You can follow up with attendees in two ways:

◆ direct follow-up by email (or phone)

◆ surveys and evaluation forms.

Email Follow-Up

You should email everyone who attended your presentation (see Tool 10.1 for a sample thank-you letter). This serves a number of purposes. It is polite and, most important, reminds participants of any steps they were supposed to take. You also want to invite their feedback and give them multiple ways to contact you.

STEP 10

The format should be similar for any type of presentation:

◆ Greet attendees personally and thank them for attending.

◆ Fulfill any commitments on your part (this includes providing links to the recording, copies of your visuals if you want to share them, and any supporting materials).

◆ Remind attendees to take action and outline the necessary steps.

◆ Offer any assistance.

◆ If directing participants elsewhere, use live links rather than just URLs. Anything they can do right away without thinking about it will increase the odds of compliance.

◆ Prepare participants for the next event or presentation.

◆ Include contact information with a real person's name and email.

POINTER

Email follow-up is great for reminding participants of action items and thanking them for attending, but it seldom gets feedback you can use unless respondents feel very strongly one way or the other. Email that comes from a real person (Cathy Johnson, as opposed to marketing) is more likely to be sent out of habit with praise, complaints, or a mix of both. Remember that feedback of any kind is a gift, even if it feels like a burden.

You also want to follow up with people who registered for the event but did not attend. Remember that if the presentation was mandatory, they will have to attend either the next event or view the recording at their convenience. If they registered voluntarily, they were interested enough in your topic to register, so you still have hope of reaching them. People often make free events a lower priority—they get wrapped up in work or lose track of time. A warmer lead than cold calling would be a shame to let go to waste. You want to connect with those missing from your audience in a way that will either get them back in the fold immediately or create an ongoing relationship that will encourage their participation in the future.

STEP 10

TOOL 10.1

Thank-You Letter

Send this letter out by email as soon as possible after the event. Remember that every minute that ticks by without participants' taking the next action step is an opportunity lost.

The usual holdup involves getting the link for the recording (if applicable). If you have all the information in advance, send it out within minutes of the webcast ending.

Dear _____:

Thank you for attending today's "Five Ways to Write Emails That Don't Annoy People" webinar. We hope you found the investment of time informative and valuable.

Because we value your opinion, we'd love to hear your feedback. Please click on the link below and answer five simple questions to help us continue to improve our education efforts.

[Provide link to evaluation.]

To thank you for your time, we have attached, with our compliments, a PDF copy of the PowerPoint visuals from the program. We know you'll find it invaluable in your endeavor to avoid poor email practices.

We at _____ are eager to assist you in the fight against communication failure. One great step would be to schedule a demonstration of our product. Contact us at _____ to arrange for a personal look at just how we can help you achieve success.

The recording of this webinar will be available within 24 hours [duration may vary depending on your platform] at [insert the link to your presentation here]. We covered a lot of information in our time together, and this provides a great way to review the content. Also please share this link with your friends and colleagues—anyone you think might benefit from seeing the presentation.

Again, thank you for attending the webinar, and we look forward to being of service to you in the future.

Sincerely,

[Insert signature of sales representative or company president.]

[List contact information.]

STEP **10**

Sending a "sorry we missed you" letter is a good way to reconnect with these people (see Tool 10.2 for an example). This letter should resemble the thank-you letter outlined above, but with a recognition that even though recipients missed the live event, they can still get the benefit of the material and content of your presentation.

Include the following in that letter:

◆ Greet the recipient.

◆ Recognize that the recipient wasn't in attendance. If participation was mandatory, don't be subtle about reminding recipients to retake the course or at least view the recording. If participation was voluntary, recognize recipients' interest in the topic and offer them the chance to benefit from the presentation despite being unable to join you live.

◆ Fulfill any obligations on your part.

◆ Remind the recipient of next steps (make any required action as easy as possible).

◆ Remind the recipient of the next event or presentation, or direct him or her to a recording of the presentation.

Surveys and Evaluations

If you have ever handed out course evaluations at the back of a classroom as people were rushing for the doors, you know you'll get results of dubious quality—they mostly reflect strong feelings one way or the other, with most of the feedback being positive and nonspecific. The only worse alternative is to hand them out and ask people to "get them back to you." Then you don't receive much feedback at all.

The good news is that many of the major platform providers, including Cisco (WebEx applications), Live Meeting, and GoToWebinar, allow you to create surveys as part of the planning for your presentation. When you schedule the presentation, you can also schedule your follow-up, thank-you letters, and surveys.

TOOL 10.2

Sorry We Missed You Letter

Send this letter out by email immediately after the web presentation is over—or at least as soon as you get the link to the recording. (You'll be amazed how many people get it and say, "Oh shoot, I forgot," but still take action or view the recording.)

Don't let the lead or the call to action go cold.

Dear _____:

Although you registered to attend today's webinar, "Five Ways to Write Email That Doesn't Annoy People," we couldn't help but notice your absence. We understand that in today's crazy work world, things come up, and you can't always attend an event even when you want to.

Fortunately, you haven't necessarily missed out on the opportunity to learn the techniques that dozens of people [or however many showed up—people love to be part of a crowd] heard. You can hear and view the recorded webinar by clicking here [include a link to the recording].

Because so many people requested them, we have also included a PDF copy of the PowerPoint visuals for you to use as a reference and share with others.

We at _____ know the topic is important to you. To get more information or to schedule a free review of your writing samples, please contact _____ at [insert a link here].

We know you'll find the recorded webinar interesting and look forward to having you join us live at our next webinar event.

Sincerely,

[Insert your signature and contact information on separate lines.]

Even if your provider doesn't have a survey feature, you can easily use SurveyMonkey (www.surveymonkey.com), Kwik Surveys (www.kwiksurveys.com), or Free Online Surveys (www.freeonline surveys.com). Plenty of others are available as well. Depending on how much detail you want to include and how many people you're surveying, you can send evaluations to every attendee's email address and receive the answers already collated and ready to review.

STEP **10**

Nothing guarantees you will get 100 percent return, but you can improve the rate and quality of your evaluations and surveys by trying the following:

◆ **Keep presentations short and relevant.** A good number of questions to use is 10—enough to give people useful data but not so many that people will resent the time spent on them. Keep the questions relevant to what you want to measure. Include a couple of questions on participants' experience with the event, a couple on your skills as the presenter, and the rest on content and application to their jobs or your outcome.

◆ **Mix up the type of questions.** Electronic templates usually allow you a mix of question types from true-or-false to multiple-choice to short-answer. Mix them up, and make sure you actually give the audience a chance to give you constructive feedback. If participants' perception of your skills was "fair," give them a short-answer box to provide you with suggestions for improvement.

◆ **Give the audience a tight (but not impossible) deadline for response.** In this electronic age, people can click on a link, fill out a survey, and get it back to you at the speed of light. Filling out a reasonable presentation evaluation form won't take long. Still, people might not be able to do it right away. Giving attendees 48 hours to complete the evaluation is a good rule of thumb—your fabulous presentation is still fresh in their minds, and they haven't completely forgotten about your request.

◆ **Make getting a certificate of completion mandatory.** Do this with caution. While it does get you a high rate of return, certification is a bit draconian and gets responses with little thought put into them. People resent having their professional development units or credit for attending held hostage. I would only use this technique in the case of training that is compulsory by law or regulation or if your stakeholders are dead set on tracking attendance.

Capture Best Practices

You have gone through a lot of hard work to get this presentation designed, rehearsed, and built, with a lot of planning and enumerable details to consider. No matter how well the presentation went, you will want to reflect on your strengths and what you still need to work on.

Worksheet 10.1 is designed to help you look at every step of this process, capture the main points, and ask yourself the questions most likely to give you good feedback. Take your time with it. Share it with trusted teammates or audience members.

Remember to be specific—"voice was good" is not helpful feedback. "Volume was good, and speaker didn't say *um*" is something you can work with. Whether giving feedback or receiving it, always ask, "So what?" Consider other, possibly better things to say in every instance and other examples to use. If you propose eliminating a question from one part of a presentation, suggest where else in the presentation it might fit.

You'll notice in the checklist a box marked "specific steps to improve performance." Don't hesitate to fill out that box immediately. Jot down any ideas that occur to you—you can edit them later when you have had time to think.

Don't be afraid to borrow ideas and best practices from other presenters. When you attend a webinar or web meeting and someone does something effective or uses a great example, make a quick note to yourself. As a screenwriter friend of mine once said, "It's not plagiarism; it's an homage." Learn from the best, add your own spin, and you'll be able to present with the best of them.

STEP **10**

Celebrate Your Accomplishments

You did it! Whether this is your very first web presentation, your first guided one, or your 500th, you have accomplished something here. If it went well, congratulations.

If it didn't go as well as you expected, I can almost guarantee it didn't go as badly as you imagined it might: You didn't have a stroke from the stress, you still have a job, and nobody (as far as you can tell) was arrested. You'll do better next time.

Take a moment and breathe. Let your body and your brain return to normal. Accept the good wishes of participants. Get up and walk away from your desk and find something cool to drink.

Plenty of time will be available to look at the feedback—good and bad. For now know that you have done something that most people don't do, at least not well, and have worked very hard to do it to the best of your ability.

Anytime now the phone will ring, and you'll get your next assignment. Maybe another class awaits, or another customer will need to see your software in action. At any rate, you know you can tackle the assignment, and each time will be easier than the time before.

This book was designed to be a reference and a workbook. Keep it somewhere handy so you can pull it out at a moment's notice.

Each time you are asked to deliver a web presentation, refer to the book for review of the checklists and templates:

◆ What have you forgotten?
◆ What didn't you do as well last time that you'd like to do better for this next demo?
◆ What worked really well that you want to make sure you keep doing?

This book promised to break down the act of web presenting into easily digested pieces that you can act on. It's up to you, now, to take action.

STEP **10**

As with any skill, you will get incrementally better at it by examining what you do now and what will make your work even more effective, and then practicing until you can do that particular action to the best of your ability. Now you just have to go for it.

It would be nice, of course, if you could read this book and not have to take all the 10 steps . . . or experience the frustrations of web presenting for yourself. At the same time, I hope you see how this can be successful, rewarding, and (dare to dream) fun.

Good luck and great presenting!

WORKSHEET 10.1
Web Presentation Self-Evaluation

This worksheet will benefit every member of the team. Each should take a good hard look at his or her work and identify what worked well and what can work better.

Complete it collectively on a conference call or at a web meeting (now that you know how to run those so well), or send it by email with a specific time frame for responses. Respondents should be as specific and clear as possible.

Step 1. Identify your objectives and outcomes

Action Item	Did You Achieve Your Goal?	How Do You Know?	Maintain, Delete, or Improve	Specific Steps to Improve Performance
Clearly defined my purpose for the presentation				
Got buy-in from all stakeholders				
Clearly defined the outcome				
Final presentation was geared to that outcome				

Step 2. Learn the platform

Action Item	Did You Achieve Your Goal?	How Do You Know?	Maintain, Delete, or Improve	Specific Steps to Improve Performance
The platform was appropriate for my purposes				
I was able to use all the appropriate functions comfortably				
The platform was appropriate for my audience				

STEP **10**

Worksheet 10.1, continued

Action Item	Did You Achieve Your Goal?	How Do You Know?	Maintain, Delete, or Improve	Specific Steps to Improve Performance
There were no problems with audience connectivity				
I chose and used all the functions appropriate for this presentation				

Step 3. Create a project plan

Action Item	Did You Achieve Your Goal?	How Do You Know?	Maintain, Delete, or Improve	Specific Steps to Improve Performance
The roles and responsibilities were assigned properly				
There were no problems meeting deadlines or assigned tasks				
The plan is usable as-is for the next project or presentation				

Step 4. Work with others

Action Item	Did You Achieve Your Goal?	How Do You Know?	Maintain, Delete, or Improve	Specific Steps to Improve Performance
I chose the appropriate people to ask for assistance				
The feedback I got was timely and useful				

Worksheet 10.1, continued

Action Item	Did You Achieve Your Goal?	How Do You Know?	Maintain, Delete, or Improve	Specific Steps to Improve Performance
There were no problems with deadlines or quality of work				
The co-presenters performed their assigned tasks flawlessly and worked well as a team				

Step 5. Create compelling content

Action Item	Did You Achieve Your Goal?	How Do You Know?	Maintain, Delete, or Improve	Specific Steps to Improve Performance
The invitation process got us the attendance we wanted				
The invitations went to the right people at the right time				
People knew what to expect as a result of the invitation				
There were no problems with registration or log-in				
The introduction was clear and focused on attaining our outcome				
We followed the introduction template effectively				

STEP 10

Worksheet 10.1, continued

Action Item	Did You Achieve Your Goal?	How Do You Know?	Maintain, Delete, or Improve	Specific Steps to Improve Performance
The "tour" of the platform was clear and useful for the audience				
The housekeeping details were appropriate and concise				
The agenda was appropriate for the audience and outcome				
The content was properly targeted to the attendees				
Examples and success stories were appropriate to this audience				

Step 6. Create visuals that support your presentation

Action Item	Did You Achieve Your Goal?	How Do You Know?	Maintain, Delete, or Improve	Specific Steps to Improve Performance
The number of visuals was appropriate				
Words in the visuals were all spelled correctly				
Visuals looked onscreen as they were designed				
Transitions, animations, and other visual aids worked properly				

STEP 10

Action Item	Did You Achieve Your Goal?	How Do You Know?	Maintain, Delete, or Improve	Specific Steps to Improve Performance
Pictures and clip art were appropriate to the audience				
Visuals appeared smoothly and quickly				
Annotation worked smoothly				
Application sharing went smoothly				

Step 7. Sharpen your presentation skills

Action Item	Did You Achieve Your Goal?	How Do You Know?	Maintain, Delete, or Improve	Specific Steps to Improve Performance
I felt comfortable presenting during the presentation				
My transitions from one visual to the next were seamless				
Annotations worked smoothly and didn't affect my concentration				
I chose the right annotation tools for each visual				
I had the appropriate level of interactivity with my audience				
I remembered to ask questions and interact at the right times				

STEP 10

Worksheet 10.1, continued

Action Item	Did You Achieve Your Goal?	How Do You Know?	Maintain, Delete, or Improve	Specific Steps to Improve Performance
The audience permissions were appropriate to my audience and my outcomes				
I displayed good verbal skills (per feedback sheet)				
I displayed good vocal skills (per feedback sheet)				

Step 8. Rehearse

Action Item	Did You Achieve Your Goal?	How Do You Know?	Maintain, Delete, or Improve	Specific Steps to Improve Performance
There were no unexpected challenges with the audience experience				
I got accurate feedback from people who watched (use the feedback forms)				
There were no unexpected problems or challenges during rehearsal				
Changes based on rehearsal were easy to make and didn't create time pressure				

STEP 10

Step 9. Present and multitask effectively

Action Item	Did You Achieve Your Goal?	How Do You Know?	Maintain, Delete, or Improve	Specific Steps to Improve Performance
I was calm and stress-free during my presentation				
I didn't lose my place or my concentration				
Any problems were invisible to the audience				
Question-and-answer session went the way I envisioned it				
The questions I planned reflected the audience's questions				
The audience came up with great questions				
The process of taking and screening audience questions worked efficiently				
My answers were targeted and concise				
I had appropriate time for question-and-answer session				
My call to action was clear				
I stated my call to action and next steps assertively and confidently				

STEP **10**

Worksheet 10.1, continued

Step 10. Follow up and keep learning

Action Item	Did You Achieve Your Goal?	How Do You Know?	Maintain, Delete, or Improve	Specific Steps to Improve Performance
The audience is responding and taking appropriate action				
The thank-you letters went out in a timely fashion				
The "sorry we missed you" letters went out in a timely fashion				
The recording was of good quality				
The recording was posted quickly, and links were included in all communication with registrants				
The evaluations measured important data				
The evaluations were sent out in a timely manner				
I got appropriate response levels to the evaluations				
The feedback I got was useful and clear				
Feedback from stakeholders was positive				
The celebratory margarita had the right amount of ice in it				

STEP 10

NOTES

_____

_____

_____

_____

_____

_____

_____

_____

_____

_____

_____

_____

_____

_____

_____

_____

_____

_____

STEP **10**

REFERENCES & RESOURCES

Because the field of web presentations is fairly new, there aren't many well-known resources and experts to draw from. A few people are establishing themselves in this area, and following are some books and websites you can look to for additional assistance as you grow your skills at presenting virtually.

Books

Clay, C. (2009). *Great webinars: How to create interactive learning that is captivating, informative and fun.* Availabe from Punchy Publishing at http://www.amazon.com/Great-Webinars-interactive-captivating-informative/dp/0976458713/ref=sr_1_1?ie=UTF8&s=books&qid=1290537483&sr=1-1

Cohan, P. (2005). *Great demo! How to create and execute stunning software demonstrations,* 2nd ed. San Jose, CA: iUniverse.

Courville, R. (2009). *The virtual presenter's handbook.* Portland, OR: CreateSpace.

Turmel, W. (2009). *6 weeks to a great webinar: Generate leads and tell your story to the world.* Glen Ellyn, IL: Achis Press.

Webinars A–Z: Your ultimate guide to online success: What are webinars and why should you care? (2010). L. A. Mondragon (Ed.). E-book available on Kindle from http://www.amazon.com/Webinars-Z-Ultimate-Success-ebook/dp/B0041D8C1G

Websites

Connected Manager: www.bnet.com/blog/virtual-manager

Conscious and Competence Theory (by W. S. Howell):
http://changingminds.org/explanations/learning/
consciousness_competence.htm

Webinar Wire: www.webinarwire.com

INDEX

webcams, 90–94
  what good visuals do, 89
vocal skills, 125–129, 134–135
Voice over Internet Protocol
  (VoIP), 23
voice quality and tone, 125–129,
  134–135

W
webcams, 32, 90
  advantages of, 92
  disadvantages of, 91–92
  dressing for, 93
  tips for using, 92–94

Weber, E., 73
WebEx, 19, 21, 28–29, 90, 100, 109,
  110, 115, 131, 140, 166
whiteboards, 26
WMV, 31
worksheets
  audience analysis, 8, 12–14
  platform comparison, 22, 36–37
  presentation outline template,
    87–88
  rehearsal feedback, 147
  self-evaluation, 172–179
  show-day, 152
  verbal and vocal skills, 134–135

Wayne Turmel is a writer, speaker, and pioneer in online presentation skills and team management. A former stand-up comedian, Wayne has parlayed his candid, humorous approach to life into a passion for helping others deal with the insanity and indignities of the modern working world—especially when it comes to technology.

Wayne has published extensively. He first contributed a chapter to the 1999 *ASTD Handbook of Training Design and Delivery* (Piskurich, Beckschi, and Hall; McGraw-Hill), the 2003 *AMA Handbook of E-Learning* (Piskurich; AMACOM Books), and *Getting the Most From Online Learning* (Piskurich; Pfeiffer), also from 2003. He's also written several books on his own including *A Philistine's Journal—An Average Guy Tackles the Classics* (New Leaf Books, 2003) and *6 Weeks to a Great Webinar* (Achis Marketing Services, 2008).

Wayne is one of the most respected management and communication voices on the web. He's a regular contributor to www.management-issues.com, the "Connected Manager" for www.bnet.com, and the host of one of the world's most popular business podcasts, "The Cranky Middle Manager Show."

After a 15-year career in training, culminating in his role as director of faculty for Communispond, he started www.greatweb meetings.com, a company dedicated to helping organizations and their people sell, facilitate, present, and manage teams through online communication and virtual communication skills.

Wayne lives in Glen Ellyn, IL, with his wife, the Duchess (Joan), Her Serene Highness (Nora), and his officemate, Byron the Demented Cockatiel.